Contents

About this book and its author

The English rendering of *'Islaam kiyaa hai!'* from Urdu which proved immensely popular and has since been printed more than a few dozen times. It explains the fundamental tenets of Islaam in easy language.

The clear exposition of the fundamental doctrines of Islaam in a simple and lucid language is remarkably admirable. .... As such it serves as a guide to the Faith of Islaam. It would give non-Muslims, who read it, a true conception of what Islaam really is.

Crescent,
Madras, 5th July 1970.

'What Islaam Is!' is an impartial and authentic study, giving the sum and substance of the Islaamic Faith in a popular style at once appealing to the reader. .... It has been written primarily to cater for the needs of those Muslim men and women who cannot afford to go through more advanced books on it due to lack of time.

The Pioneer,
Lucknow, 1st May 1965.

THE AUTHOR OF this book, Maulana Muhammad Manzoor No'maanii, is a well known religious scholar and one of the leading lights of the Tabliigh and Diinii Ta'liim movements in India. He has rendered yeoman service to Muslims of India through his writings in Urdu, which seek to popularise the correct teachings of religion.

This small treatise can be called "A handbook of basic Islaam." In its twenty three chapters, written in an easy and captivating language and heart-to-heart style, with quotations from the Qur-aan and ahaadiith (traditions of the Prophet — Peace be upon him), the author has succeeded in putting in a nutshell all that a man is desirous of wanting to know about the fundamental beliefs and practices of Islaam. Another remarkable feature of the book is the inclusion therein of selected prayers taken from the Qur-aan and traditions, which, efficacious as they are, leave no seeker of truth untouched by their burning sincerity.

No wonder the Urdu version of this book has emerged as a best seller with over forty editions. The English version is being taught as a text book to English speaking Muslim children in several countries.

بسم الله الرحمن الرحيم

In the Name of Allah the Most Beneficent the Most Merciful

What Islaam Is!

What Islaam Is!

being a translation of
Maulana Muhammad Manzoor No'maanii's
Islaam kiyaa hai?

by
Muhammad Aasif Kidwai
M.A. PH.D.

Adam Publishers & Distributors
New Delhi -2 (India)

MAXIMUM RETAIL PRICE
INCLUSIVE OF ALL TAXES
₹80

ADAM PUBLISHERS & DISTRIBUTORS
Exporters & Importers
1542, Pataudi House, Darya Ganj,
New Delhi-110002
Phone (0) : 3271690, 3282550
Fax: 3267510 (R) 91- 4553953

e-mail:apd@bol.net. in
www.adampublishers.com

IInd Edition 2002

ISBN : 81-7435-130 - 6

Style & Designed by
Graphic Time Computers
1406. G. St. K. Mehal D. Ganj. N. Delhi-2 Ph. 3250836

Printed & Bound in India Published by
S. Sajid Ali for
ADAM PUBLISHERS & DISTRIBUTORS
1542, Pataudi House, Darya Ganj,
New Delhi-110002

Preface

In the Name of Allah, the Most Benevolent, the Most Merciful

SHOULD IT BE POSSIBLE for the noble Prophet (Peace be upon him) to be sent down into the world once again by Allah, what would his reaction be on seeing the conduct and behaviour and the general design of life of the community that passes today by the name of Muslim? And what advice and command would he give to such of his followers who still possess in their hearts some solicitude for Faith and whose souls have not yet frozen to Islaam?

Without the least hesitation I can say that he will be extremely pained at the spectacle of utter moral and spiritual degeneration among the bulk of Muslims present these days, as much as he was by the brutal treatment meted out to him by the people of Taa-if or by the savage assaults made by the callous polytheists at Uhud. And his message to earnest and devoted Muslims who are blessed with a genuine concern for Faith will be to dedicate themselves whole-heartedly to the task of improving and reforming the lamentable religious state of his ummah and breathing into it again the spirit of Faith and an Islaamic way of life.

So, if you find yourself in agreement with me and your heart concurs with what I have said, you must resolve, here and now, and in all sincerity, to make this endeavour a part of your life. For my part, I am absolutely confident that it is the choicest way to earn the good pleasure of the Lord and the blessings of the Prophet (Peace be upon him) and make his soul happy.

By the grace of Allah, efforts for the moral and religious revival of Muslims are being made on a fairly large scale in India and Pakistan and in several other countries, also, in the form of a movement called Tabliigh. Wherever you may be living you can take part in this effort,

i

according to your means and circumstances, along with other earnest sons of Islaam of your place, and, also, do what you can individually in respect of it.

This small book which is now in your hands is a part of this endeavour. It has been written specially to meet the needs of Muslim men and women who do not know much about Islaam or who cannot avail themselves of more advanced books on it. They can read it themselves or have it read out to them by others, and also communicate its contents to their bretheren by reading the book publicly in masjids (mosques) and at other Muslim congregations, and, thus, do their bit towards their own religious correction and reform as well as that of others.

Though the book consists only of about one hundred and fifty pages, the sum and substance of the Faith has been covered fully in it. Within its twenty lessons all those teachings of the Qur-aan and ahaadith (traditions) have been compressed by knowing which, and by acting upon which, a common man cannot only become a good Muslim, but a perfect man of Faith and a 'friend' of the Lord also. Besides, it can be freely presented to non-Muslims who may be interested in knowing about Islaam and its precepts.

The humble author could only produce the book and that he has done. Now, to make it serve the purpose, in a worthwhile manner, for which it has been written, depends solely on your choice and co-operation. Had his financial resources permitted, the author would have got it printed in millions and sent a copy of it, free of cost, to every educated Muslim in India. The conditions now prevailing in India particularly cry out for it. But, from the beginning, it has been the Will of Allah that those who cherish such aspirations seldom have the means to realise them — and, without doubt, there lies the great wisdom of the Lord in it also.

Be that as it may, it is beyond the power of the writer to fulfil this desire. But, if Muslims in whose hands the book may reach decide, in their eagerness to propitiate the Lord and give happiness to the soul of the Prophet (Peace be upon him) and to earn for themselves a bountiful reward in the hereafter, to make it available, or its contents, to as many of their bruthren as possible, the real aim of its writing and publication can be fulfilled to a great extent.

As it has been indicated already, in the new context of things in India the religious future of Muslims rests, apparently, on the sole condition that every follower of the Prophet (Peace be upon him) here, who is alive to the importance of the Faith and knows what it means, makes it a personal duty to strive for the Islaamic regeneration for the general body of Muslims and a mission of his life to carry the message of Faith and the teachings of Islaam to each and every member of his community.

Allah is the One that grants success and He is the One from Whom we seek assistance.

Muhammad Manzoor No'maanii,

10th Ramadaan 1369.
Lucknow, India

Note:
- In the first few lessons reference of the ahaadith has been given. In later lessons this was not deemed necessary, as all the other ahaadith are taken from the Mishkaatul Masaabiih.
- In the ahaadith and some Qur-aanic translations, for the ease of readers, literal meanings of the original Arabic have been given. Word for word translations has been avoided.

iii

The virtues of acquiring knowledge

BROTHERS, − YOU ALL WILL, perhaps, be aware that Islaam is not the name of a caste or community so that anyone who is born in it automatically becomes a Muslim without having to do anything, on his own part, about it just as a child born in a Sha<u>ykh</u> or Sayyid family becomes a Sha<u>ykh</u> or a Sayyid, as a matter of course, and there is nothing it can do in this regard.

Islaam, on the other hand, is the name of the Faith and way of life which was brought into the world from Allah by His true and devoted Apostle, the Prophet Mu<u>h</u>ammad (Peace be upon him), and is preserved to this day, in its pristine purity in the Qur-aan and the holy a<u>h</u>aadii<u>th</u> (traditions). Thus, he alone can be called a Muslim who accepts that Faith and practises that way of life. Those who are ignorant of the teachings of Islaam, or do not act upon them, are not true Muslims by any means. We, therefore, conclude that two things are necessary for anyone to be a true Muslim:

Firstly, to acquire a proper knowledge of the teachings of Islaam, or, at least, of its basic and fundamental doctrines;

And, secondly, to believe in these teachings as true and to resolve sincerely to live according to them.

This, in sum, is what Islaam is. To acquire knowledge of the tenets of Islaam, i.e., its essential teachings is the first requisite of being a Muslim. A <u>h</u>adii<u>th</u> (tradition) of the Prophet (Peace be upon him) reads:

"To acquire knowledge of the Faith is the duty of all Muslims."
− Ibn Maajah, Bayhaqii.

It is necessary to bear constantly in mind that to carry out what is described in the religion as a duty is an act of worship in Islaam. To exert oneself for the sake of obtaining an adequate Faith, hence, is also an act of worship on which there is a bountiful reward from the Lord. The noble Prophet (Peace be upon him) has proclaimed great merit in it. Take these ahaadiith (traditions), for instance:

"He who goes forth in search of religious knowledge engages himself in the cause of Allah until he returns." — Tirmidhii.

"For him who goes out in search of religious knowledge Allah shall make easy the way to Heaven." — Muslim.

"Thirst for religious knowledge and the pursuit of it atones for one's previous sins." — Tirmidhii.

In short, the cultivation of religious knowledge, i.e., the knowledge of the essential teachings of Islaam, is binding on all Muslims, rich and poor, educated and uneducated, male and female, old and young. From the ahaadiith (traditions) of the Prophet (Peace be upon him) quoted above, we also learn that a rich reward awaits us in the hereafter for the time spent and the pains taken for the sake of it. Let us all now make up our minds that we will strive earnestly to equip ourselves with adequate knowledge of Faith and a proper understanding of the basic doctrine of Islaam.

For Muslims who, on account of their age or occupation, cannot join a Muslim theological institution and take a regular course of Islaamic religious instruction, the best thing will be that, if they are educated, they should develop the habit of reading reliable books on Islaam regularly, and if they are not or only nominally so, they should have such books read out to them by others who can read and understand. If the custom of reading religious books, individually or in groups, can become common in Muslim homes and masaajid (mosques), and at their other gatherings, the spread of religious knowledge to all classes and sections of the community will be greatly facilitated indeed.

vi

This small book has been written solely to fulfil this purpose. All the necessary information regarding Islaam and the teachings of the sacred Prophet (Peace be upon him), which a Muslim ought to possess, has been furnished in it in a simple language. Let us all learn these truths and precepts ourselves and impart them to others as well and make it a mission of our lives to popularise them in the world. A hadiith (tradition) of the Prophet (Peace be upon him) says:

"If a person engages himself in the pursuit of Islaamic religious knowledge with the object of reviving the Faith through it (i.e., by instructing it to others and bringing them round to act on it) and he dies in the process, his place will be so very close to the Prophets (Peace be upon them) in the hereafter that there will be only a difference of one degree between them and him." — Daarimii.

May Allah grant us the great good fortune of learning the precepts of Islaam ourselves and teaching them to others, and of acting on them and endeavouring sincerely to persuade others to do the same.

Lesson 1

The Kalimah

لَا اِلٰهَ اِلَّا اللهُ مُحَمَّدُ رَّسُوْلُ اللهِ

'Laa ilaaha illal-laahu Muhammadur rasu-lullaah'

There is no deity (who is worthy of worship and obedience)
save One Allah, and Muhammad is His Apostle.

BROTHERS, — THIS CONFESSION is the gateway to Islaam, the
arch-stone of Faith. By affirming it and reciting it with sincerity and
conviction, even a life-long heathen or polytheist can become a
Muslim, a man of Faith and earn his title to salvation. The condition,
however, is that he should have accepted conscientiously and with
full understanding, the declaration of the Oneness of Allah and the
Apostleship of the Prophet Muhammad (Peace be upon him)
contained in it. Thus, anyone who repeats the confession mechani-
cally, without understanding it and without knowing what the
concepts of Divine Unity and Apostleship and Prophecy mean, will
not gain recognition in the sight of Allah as a Muslim. It is, therefore,
necessary to study its meaning and implications carefully.

The confession consists of two parts. The first part 'Laa ilaaha
illal-laah' contains the affirmation of the Oneness of Allah.

It means that no one except the Almighty is worthy of worship
and obedience. Worship and obeisance should be offered to Him
alone because He and no one else is our Lord and Creator, Nourisher,
Sustainer, Dispenser of Life and Death, sickness and health, poverty
and riches. In short, all manner of good and evil, gain or loss, lies
solely in His control. Apart from Him, whatever living things exist on
the earth, or in the heavens, be they men or angels, are all His
creatures and slaves. He is partnered by no one, no one has a share in
His Divinity nor can anyone amend or alter His Will or interfere with
His function. Hence, He and He alone is worthy of devotion and

1

worship. He alone is the Supreme Being, the Glorious One, to whom all our prayers and supplications should be addressed. He alone is the real Owner of the heavens and the earth, the Monarch of monarchs, the Lord Sovereign. It is, therefore, necessary that all His commands and injunctions are strictly obeyed and faithfully carried out. As against His commands, the commands of no one should be heeded to, no matter whether they are of our parents or rulers or of the head of the community or a dear friend, or the bidding of our own heart. In a nutshell, when once we have realised and confessed the truth that Allah alone, and no one besides Him, is worthy of worship and obedience, our conduct should also be in conformity with it, so much so that anyone who sees us should know by our behaviour that we are the devoted servants of the Lord who carry out His commands dutifully and live and die for His sake alone.

Brothers, — this 'Laa ilaaha illal-laah' is the keystone of Islaam and the first and foremost item in the teachings of all the Prophets (Peace be upon them). It commands the highest, the most important place in the religious scheme of things. A famous hadiith (tradition) of the Prophet (Peace be upon him) reads:

"There are more than seventy departments of Faith and among them the most superior and exalted is belief in the kalimah of 'Laa ilaaha illal-laah'." — Bukhaa-rii, Sahiih Muslim.

For this reason, among the dhikr[1] (prayer-formulas) it is also the best. States the noble Prophet (Peace be upon him):

"Of all the prayer-formulas the best and most excellent is that of 'Laa ilaaha illal-laah'." — Ibn Maajah, Nasa-ee.

In another hadiith (tradition) it is related that once Allah gave this reply to a question put to Him by Prophet Musaa (Moses) (Peace be upon him):

---

1. The word dhikr (remembrance) which occurs in the original literally means a special phrase meant for recitation by the devout. — Translator.

"O Musaa (Moses), if the seven heavens and the seven earths and all that is contained in them are placed on one side of the balance and 'Laa ilaaha illal-laah' on the other, the side on which 'Laa ilaaha illal-laah' is placed will turn out to be heavier." — Sharhus Sunnah.

Brothers, — the unique virtue and excellence of 'Laa ilaaha illal-laah' is due solely to the fact that it contains the solemn affirmation of Divine Unity, the assertion, the pledge and the declaration that we shall worship Him alone and offer our homage and obeisance to no one apart from Him, and shall make Him the sole pivot of our existence. It, indeed, is the life-breath of Islaam. That is why, the noble Prophet (Peace be upon him) has advised Muslims to refresh and reinvigorate their Faith by repeating the kalimah frequently.

It is narrated that the Prophet (Peace be upon him) once said, "O men! keep on refreshing your Faith." Upon this the Companions enquired, "O Prophet of Allah! How are we to do so?" The Prophet (Peace be upon him) replied, "by reciting the kalimah much and often." — Musnad Ahmad, Jam'ul Fawaa-id.

The kalimah 'Laa ilaaha illal-laah' holds the power to restore and revitalise the Faith for the simple reason that it embodies the affirmation of Divine Unity and the covenant to worship Allah alone, to do allegiance to no one aside of Him, and to hold Him dearer and nearer to the heart than anything or anybody else in the world. As we have said earlier, it is the essence, the sustaining principle of Islaam. So, the more we will utter it attentively, concentrating duly on what it stands for, the more will our Faith gain in vitality and our covenant in strength, and our whole life will, In-Sha-Allah, get cast in the mould of 'Laa ilaaha illal-laah'.

The second part

The second part of the kalimah consist of 'Muhammadur rasu-lullaah'. In it the affirmation is made of the divine apostleship of the Prophet Muhammad (Peace be upon him). That the Prophet Muhammad (Peace be upon him) is the Apostle of Allah means that he was raised up by the Almighty for the guidance of the world, and whatever he taught, preached or revealed, like the Divinity of the origin of the Qur-aan, the existence of the angels, the certainty of the last day, the resurrection, the judgement, the award of Heaven and Hell acccording to one's deeds on earth, was one hundred per cent true and authentic. Indeed, the apostleship of the holy Prophet (Peace be upon him) denotes nothing more and nothing less than this, that all the things he taught to the world, all the truths he revealed to mankind, were based on divine inspiration, that they were based on special and authoritative knowledge vouchsafed to him by Allah, and so they were absolutely correct and beyond dispute. There is not the least excuse, the slightest reason, for doubting or questioning his word. The guidance he gave to men, the laws he laid down, were Divine Guidance and Divine Laws that had been inspired to him by the Almighty. You would have realised that the acceptance of anyone as a divine apostle automatically implies that each and every precept and command of his should be whole-heartedly believed in and obeyed, for Allah raised up His Apostle in the world solely to convey, through him to mankind, the commands and precepts He wanted it to follow. Says the Qur-aan:

"We sent not an Apostle, but to be obeyed in accordance with the Will of Allah." — Surah Nisaa (IV), 64.

To believe in anyone as an Apostle and to accept him as such, thus, means simply to hold every word of his as true, to regard his teachings and guidance to be the teachings and guidance of Allah, and to decide, once and for all, to lead one's life according to the precepts he taught. So if a person recites the kalimah but does not, as a logical consequence of it, resolve firmly to hold all the teachings of the Prophet (Peace be upon him) to be wholly true and all that may run counter to them to be wholly false, and to abide by his sharii'ah (holy law) and his commands faithfully, he, of course, is not a man of Faith and a Muslim. He, probably, has not even understood what it means to be a Muslim.

4

It is obvious that once we have recited the kalimah and accepted the Prophet (Peace be upon him) as the true Apostle of Allah, it becomes obligatory for us to believe in his guidance, to adhere to his commands and to observe faithfully the sharii'ah he brought.

A covenant

From the meaning and interpretation of the holy kalimah given above, you will have realised that it is a covenant. It embodies the pledge and the vow that we believe in Allah as the One and Only Lord Sovereign, Master and Creator, and regard everything that exists in this world and the hereafter to be exclusively in His control, and that, since we do so, we will worship Him alone and carry out His commands the way a servant and a slave carries out the commands of his master, and love Him and adore Him above all else, and, further, that we accept Prophet Muhammad (Peace be upon him) as the true Apostle of Allah and will abide by his guidance as a loyal follower and fashion our lives according to the holy law laid down by him. In fact, Faith denotes nothing except this pledge and covenant and this is precisely what the affirmation of Divine Unity and apostleship means.

A Muslim should, therefore, hold himself bound by this covenant and try his level best to shape his conduct in its light so that he may earn recognition in the eyes of Allah as a genuine man of Faith and attain his salvation and place in Paradise.

Those who are blessed enough to bear Faith honestly in both the parts of the holy kalimah, and to give proof of it by word as well as by deed, are the recipients of countless glad tidings like the one reproduced below:

"It is related by Sayyidina Anas that the Prophet (Peace be upon him) once said to Sayyidina Mu'aadh, 'Allah has forbidden the Fire of Hell for him who affirms the kalimah of 'Muhammadur rasu-lullaah' with a true heart'." — Bukhaa-rii, Sahiih Muslim.

5

Brothers, — affirm 'Laa ilaaha illal-laah Mu<u>h</u>ammadur rasu-lullaah' with a true heart and with full knowledge and awareness of its implications and importance, and resolve now and forever to lead your lives according to it in order that your attestation may not turn out to be false. On this very attestation depends your Faith and salvation.

Lesson 2

Salaah

THE FIRST AND MOST IMPORTANT duty in Islaam, after one has brought Faith in Allah and in the Prophet Muhammad (Peace be upon him) and borne witness to Divine Oneness and the apostleship of the noble Prophet (Peace be upon him), is salaah. It is a most special act of Divine Worship which a Muslim is called upon to perform five times a day. There are numerous verses of the Qur-aan and the ahaadiith (traditions) of the august Prophet (Peace be upon him) enjoining salaah upon us. It has been described as the pillar and foundation of Faith.

If salaah is offered with a sincere heart and proper devotion and mental concentration, it is particularly vested with the property of cleansing the heart and reforming one's life and ridding it of sins and impurities. It generates love for piety and truth and promotes fear of Allah in man. Thus it is that Islaam has laid greater emphasis on it than on any other religious obligation. When anyone came to the Prophet (Peace be upon him) to embrace Islaam, the first promise the sacred Prophet (Peace be upon him) took from him after instructing him in Divine Oneness, was that he will offer salaah regularly. In any case, after the kalimah, salaah is the bedrock of Islaam.

Ahaadiith (traditions)

We know from the ahaadiith (traditions) that the august Prophet (Peace be upon him) used to equate neglect of salaah with infidelity. He denounced it as the way of the unbelievers. He would say that those who did not offer salaah had no share in the Faith.

7

"A ḥadiith (tradition) of the Prophet (Peace be upon him) reads, 'What separates a Believer from infidelity is simply the ṣalaah'." — Saḥiih Muslim.

This ḥadiith (tradition) clearly warns that if a Muslim will give up ṣalaah he will be associated with infidelity; his conduct will become the conduct of an infidel. In another ḥadiith (tradition), the Prophet (Peace be upon him) has said, "He has no share in Islaam who does not offer ṣalaah." — Durre Manthuur with reference to Musnad Bazzaar.

And here is another ḥadiith (tradition) from which we can imagine what a great act of virtue and felicity it is to offer ṣalaah regularly and how utterly fatal and ruinous it is to neglect it. Once, while urging upon the Muslims to be most particular about ṣalaah, the sacred Prophet (Peace be upon him) is reported to have observed:

"Whoever will offer ṣalaah properly and regularly, it will be for him on the Last Day a source of light, a proof of his Faith and a means to salvation. (On the other hand) whoever will not offer it carefully and regularly, it will be for him neither a source of light nor a proof of Faith nor a means to salvation, and the end of such a person will be with Qaa-ruun[1] Fir'aun[2], Haa-maan[3] and Ubai bin Khalaf[4]" — Musnad Aḥmad.

Brothers, — let us now imagine what our end is going to be if we failed to cultivate the habit of offering ṣalaah correctly and regularly.

---

(1) Same as Korah. — Translator.
(2) Pharaoh. — Translator.
(3) Name of Pharaoh's waziir (minister). — Translator.
(4) One of the bitterest enemies of the noble Prophet (Peace be upon him) in Makkah.
    — Translator.

8

The ignominy and disgrace of the defaulters on the Last Day

The ignominy and disgrace the defaulters of salaah will have to suffer at the very outset on the Day of Judgement has been spoken of in these words in the Qur-aan:

"The day that the shin shall be laid bare, and they shall be summoned to bow in adoration, but they shall not be able, their eyes will be cast down — ignominy will cover them, seeing that they had been summoned aforetime to bow in adoration while they were whole (and had refused)." — Surah Qalam (LXVIII), 42,43.

The verse tells that on the Last Day, when the hour of judgement will arrive, (when all mystery will vanish and reality will be fully manifest), and every man and woman born into the world from the first day to the last will be raised up again and gathered together, Allah will reveal Himself to them in full glory and splendour. Everyone will then be called upon to bow in adoration before Allah. The fortunate and the faithful among them who had been regular in their salaah in the world and were, thus, accustomed to kneeling down before the Lord will, at once, bow down in adoration, but those who, in spite of being healthy and strong, had not observed salaah in their lifetime, will find that their backs had suddenly grown stiff like a board and they will remain standing with the infidels, unable to bend down and carry out the prostration. They will be covered with ignominy, their eyes will be downcast, they will not be able even to look up. Before the chastisement of Hell, they will have to bear the chastisement of humiliation and disgrace. May Allah, by His grace, save us all from it!.

In truth, a habitual defaulter of salaah is a sort of a rebel against Allah and deserves all the humiliation and punishment that may be meted out to him. According to some legists of Islaam, a Muslim who rejects salaah is liable to be punished with death, like an apostate.

Brothers, — we must realise it thoroughly and well that without salaah the claim to Islaam is altogether meaningless.

9

Salaah alone is the Islaamic act that joins us with Allah and makes us deserving of His grace.

Blessings of salaah

When a person stands before the Almighty with his arms folded, five times a day, and celebrates His praises and kneels down before Him and touches the ground with his forehead and makes earnest supplications to Him, he becomes worthy of His love and beneficence, his sins are forgiven with every salaah he offers, his heart attains enlightenment and his life becomes pure. The Prophet (Peace be upon him) once gave an excellent example to illustrate the truth.

"He asked his Companions, 'Tell me, if a stream flows at the door of anyone of you and he takes a dip in it five times a day, will any grime be left on his body?.' The Companions replied, 'No Sir. No grime will be left on his body.' The Prophet (Peace be upon him) said, 'It is exactly the same with the five daily prayers. Allah removes all impurities and sins because of their auspiciousness'." — Bukhaa-rii, Sahiih Muslim.

Superiority of congregation

It appears from the Prophet's (Peace be upon him) ahaadiith (traditions) that salaah should be offered in congregation if one wants to derive full benefit from it. The Prophet (Peace be upon him) was so very particular about it that, once, while condemning the conduct of those who avoided coming to the masjid (mosque) to say their prayers in congregation due to laziness or indifference, he observed angrily that he felt like burning down their homes. — Muslim.

This one hadiith (tradition) is enough to show how repugnant it is to Allah and the Prophet (Peace be upon him) that anyone should not offer his prayers in congregation. Another hadiith (tradition) says:-

"The reward on saying salaah in congregation is twenty seven times as much as saying it alone."[1]. — Bukhaa-rii, Sahiih Muslim.

Apart from the reward in the hereafter, there are many other advantages in offering salaah in congregation. For instance, one acquires the habit of punctuality by attending the masjid (mosque) regularly to say his prayers in congregation; it enables Muslim brethren of the locality to assemble at one place five times every day and this can be turned to great benefit; the practice of saying salaah regularly in the masjid congregationally makes a man thoroughly regular in his prayers, for it has been seen that those who offer their prayers individually at home are often inclined to be neglectful. Yet another notable advantage in saying the prayers in congregation is that the salaah of each participant becomes a part of the salaah of the whole congregation in which, along with others, there are also generally present some venerable and virtuous servants of Allah, whose salaah is of a very high order. Their salaah finds acceptance with Allah and the expectation from His Benevolent Grace is that when He will grant acceptance to the prayers of some members of the congregation He will, along with them, accept the prayers of the rest of the congregation too.

Now, imagine what rich rewards and blessings do we deprive ourselves of when we do not go to the masjid (mosque) to offer our prayers in congregation without a valid excuse.

---

1. It should be noted that the superiority of offering salaah in congregation is only for men. The ahaadiith (traditions) say clearly that women earn greater reward on saying their prayers at home than in the masjid (mosque).

Meekness and humility

The offering of salaah with meekness and humility means that, believing Allah to be Omnipresent and All- Seeing, the salaah should be offered in such a way that the heart is filled with His love and stricken with awe by the thought of His Greatness and Magnificence, as if a criminal was standing in front of a great judge or a mighty ruler. As a devotee stands up for salaah he should visualise that he is standing in the presence of the Almighty, out of reverence to Him. When he bows his head in ruku',[1] or kneels down to perform the sajdah,[2] he should imagine that it was all being carried out in front of Allah and in expression of his own utter worthlessness and humility. Better still, whatever is recited during salaah, whether while standing or in ruku' or sajdah, should be done with a proper understanding of its meaning. The real joy and beauty of salaah is experienced only when it is offered with an intelligent appreciation of its contents. It is not at all difficult to learn the meaning of surahs[3] that are generally recited in salaah.

The devotion of the heart and the sentiments of awe and humbleness, indeed, are the very soul of salaah. The ultimate success and deliverance of believers who offer such a kind of salaah is assured. Declares the Qur-aan:-

"The believers must [eventually] win through-those who humble themselves in their prayers." — *Surah Mu-minuun (XXIII) 1-2.*

Says the Prophet (Peace be upon him), "Allah has made the five daily prayers obligatory. Whoever did the wudu[4] properly and offered his prayers at the right time and carried out ruku' and sajdah as they ought to be, humbly and reverentially, for him the promise of Allah is that he will be pardoned; and whoever did not do so (i.e., did

---

1. Bowing low. — Translator.
2. Prostration. — Translator.
3. Chapters of the Qur-aan. — Translator.
4. Ablution performed before saying prayers. — Translator.

not say his prayers in this manner), for him there is no such promise. Allah will pardon or punish him as He will please." — Musnad Ahmad, Sunan Abu Daawuud.

Method

When the time for prayers comes, we should perform wudu carefully, believing that this washing and cleansing was necessary before we presented ourselves before the Lord and worshipped Him. The Almighty, in His benevolence, has invested wudu with great auspiciousness. The sins and transgressions of the parts of the body that are washed during it, are forgiven because of it. The unholy effects of sins are, so to speak, washed away by the water used in wudu. As, after wudu, we stand up for salaah, the predominant thought in our minds should be that we, the sinning and defaulting slaves, were going to stand before a Lord and Master from whom nothing was concealed, who knew all about us, the hidden as well as the manifest, and before whom we would have to appear on the Day of Judgement. We should then formulate precisely the intention to offer the particular prayer and raising the hands up to our ears, pronounce not only with the tongue but with our hearts, too, the formula:

$$ اَللّٰهُ اَكْبَرْ $$

[Transcription: Allahu Akbar.]

Allah is Great.

After it, with arms folded across the chest, and a full awareness of the fact of our presence before the Almighty, we should recite:

$$ سُبْحَانَكَ اللّٰهُمَّ وَبِحَمْدِكَ وَتَبَارَكَ اسْمُكَ وَتَعَالَى جَدُّكَ $$

$$ وَلَا إِلٰهَ غَيْرُكَ $$

13

[Transcription: Sub<u>h</u>aana-kall-laa-humma wa bi<u>h</u>amdika wa tabaa-rakas-muka wa-ta'aala jadduka walaa ilaaha <u>gh</u>ayruka].

O Allah, with Thy glorification and Thy praise; blessed is Thy name, great is Thy glory, and there is no deity except Thee.

اَعُوْذُ بِاللهِ مِنَ الشَّيْطٰنِ الرَّجِيْمِ ، بِسْمِ اللهِ الرَّحْمٰنِ الرَّحِيْمِ

[Transcription: A'oo-<u>dh</u>u billahi-mina<u>sh</u> <u>sh</u>aytaanir rajiim. Bismillaahir ra<u>h</u>maa-nir ra<u>h</u>iim.]

I seek refuge in Allah from the wicked devil and begin with the name of Allah, the Most Benevolent, the All - Merciful.

اَلْحَمْدُ لِلّٰهِ رَبِّ الْعَالَمِيْنَ ٥ اَلرَّحْمٰنِ الرَّحِيْمِ ٥ مَالِكِ يَوْمِ الدِّيْنِ ٥ اِيَّاكَ نَعْبُدُ وَاِيَّاكَ نَسْتَعِيْنُ ٥ اِهْدِنَا الصِّرَاطَ الْمُسْتَقِيْمَ ٥ صِرَاطَ الَّذِيْنَ اَنْعَمْتَ عَلَيْهِمْ ٥ غَيْرِ الْمَغْضُوبِ عَلَيْهِمْ وَلَا الضَّالِّيْنَ ٥ اٰمِيْن

[Transcription: Al<u>h</u>amdu lillaahi rab-bil 'aa-lamiin, ar-ra<u>h</u>maan-nir ra<u>h</u>iim, maaliki yaumid diin, iyyaaka na'budu wa iyyaaka nas-ta'een, ihdinas <u>s</u>iraa<u>t</u>al mustaqiim, <u>s</u>iraa<u>t</u>al la<u>dh</u>iina an'amta 'alayhim, <u>gh</u>ayril ma<u>gh</u>duubi 'alayhim wa-la<u>d</u>-<u>d</u>aal-liin. Aa-miin.]

"Praise be to Allah, Lord of the worlds, the Compassionate, the Merciful, Owner of the Day of Judgement. Thee alone do we worship, and to Thee alone do we beg for help. Show us the straight path: the path of those whom Thou has favoured; not (the path) of those who earn Thine anger nor of those who go astray. Aa-miin!" — *Surah Faati-<u>h</u>ah (I).*

Then some other surah of the Qur-aan, or a part thereof, should be recited. Here we give four brief surahs along with their translations.

14

وَالْعَصْرِ ٥ إِنَّ الْإِنْسَانَ لَفِي خُسْرٍ ٥ إِلَّا الَّذِينَ آمَنُوا وَعَمِلُوا الصَّالِحَاتِ وَتَوَاصَوْا بِالْحَقِّ وَتَوَاصَوْا بِالصَّبْرِ .

[Transcription: Wal'asr, innal insaana lafii khusr, illal ladhiina aa-manuu wa'a-milus saali-haati wa-tawaasau bil-haq-qi wa-tawaasau bis-sabri.]

"By the Time! Lo, man is in a state of great loss, save those who believe and do good deeds, and exhort one another to truth, and exhort one another to patient perseverance." — Surah 'Asr (CIII).

قُلْ هُوَ اللهُ أَحَدٌ ٥ اَللهُ الصَّمَدُ ٥ لَمْ يَلِدْ وَلَمْ يُولَدْ ٥ وَلَمْ يَكُنْ لَّهُ كُفُوًا أَحَدٌ .

[Transcription: Qul huwal-laahu ahad, alla-hus samad, lam yalid, wa-lam yuu-lad wa-lam yakul lahu kufu-wan a-had.]

"Say: 'It is Allah, the Unique! Allah, the eternally besought of all! He begetteth not nor was begotten. And there is none comparable unto Him!'." — Surah Ikh-laas (CXII).

قُلْ أَعُوذُ بِرَبِّ الْفَلَقِ ٥ مِنْ شَرِّ مَا خَلَقَ ٥ وَمِنْ شَرِّ غَاسِقٍ إِذَا وَقَبَ ٥ وَمِنْ شَرِّ النَّفَّاثَاتِ فِي الْعُقَدِ ٥ وَمِنْ شَرِّ حَاسِدٍ إِذَا حَسَدَ ٥

[Transcription: Qul a-'oodhu bi-rabbil falaq, min sharri maa khalaq, wa-min sharri ghaa-siqin i-dhaa waqab, wa-min sharrin naffaa-thaa-ti fil 'u-qad, wa-min sharri haa-si-din i-dhaa hasad.]

"Say: 'I seek refuge in the Lord of the Dawn from the mischief of created things; from the mischief of Darkness as it over-spreads; from mischief of those who practise secret arts; and from the mischief of the envious one as he practises envy'." — Surah Falaq (CXIII).

قُلْ أَعُوذُ بِرَبِّ النَّاسِ ٥ مَلِكِ النَّاسِ ٥ إِلٰهِ النَّاسِ ٥ مِنْ شَرِّ

الْوَسْوَاسِ الْخَنَّاسِ ٥ الَّذِيْ يُوَسْوِسَ فِيْ صُدُوْرِ النَّاسِ ٥
مِنَ الْجِنَّةِ وَالنَّاسِ ٥

[Transcription: Qul a-'oo-dhu bi-rabbin naas, malikin naas, ilaahin naas, min sharril was-waasil khan-naas, al-ladhii yuu-was-wisu fii suduurin naas, minal jinnati wan-naas.]

"Say: 'I seek refuge in the Lord and Cherisher of mankind, the King (or Ruler) of mankind, the Allah (or Judge) of mankind, from the mischief of the sneaking whisperer who withdraws (after his whisper) - (the same) who whispers into the hearts of mankind - among jinns and among men'." — Surah Naas (CXIV).

Anyhow, after the Surah Faati-hah (Alhamdulillaahi rabbil 'aa-la-miin) some other surah of the Qur-aan, or a part of it, is to be recited. Only this much of the Qur-aan is recited during each rak'ah of salaah. When the recitation has been completed, with the thought of the Majesty and Glory of the Lord embedded in our hearts, we should say 'Allahu Akbar' and perform ruku' by placing our hands on our knees without bending them and repeat a number of times the phrase:

سُبْحَانَ رَبِّيَ الْعَظِيْمِ

[Transcription: Subhaana rabbiyal 'aziim].

Glory be to my Lord, the most Elevated.

While reciting the above formula in ruku' we should also meditate on its meaning, on the Glory and the Magnificence of the Lord, then the head be raised from the ruku', saying:

سَمِعَ اللهُ لِمَنْ حَمِدَهُ

[Transcription: Sami'al-laahu liman hami-dah]

Allah has heard the servant who has praised Him.

$$رَبَّنَا لَكَ الْحَمْدُ$$

[Transcription: Rab-ba-naa lakal hamd.]

Our Lord! Praise be to Thee.

Then, again, we should say 'Allahu Akbar' from the depth of our hearts, and prostrate ourselves before the Lord and perform two sajdahs simultaneously. During the sajdah, the under-mentioned formula should be repeated a number of times imagining inwardly that Allah was present right there, seeing and hearing everything, and we were addressing the words directly to Him.

$$سُبْحَانَ رَبِّيَ الْأَعْلٰى$$

[Transcription: Sub-haa-na rab-bi-yal aa'laa.]

Glory be to my Lord, the Most High.

While reciting these words in sajdah, also, we should try sincerely to call forth within ourselves the realisation of our abject helplessness and humility and the Supreme Might and Magnificence of the Lord. The deeper and stronger the realisation, the better the truer the salaah, for this sentiment constitutes the very life and soul of worship. This completes one rak'ah. All the remaining rak'ahs are to be offered similarly, except that 'Sub-haa-na-kal laa-hum-ma' is recited only in the first rak'ah.

When we sit during salaah, or at the end of it, we recite 'At-ta-hiy-yaat' which is its very essence and substance:

$$اَلتَّحِيَّاتُ لِلّٰهِ وَالصَّلَوَاتُ وَالطَّيِّبَاتُ ، اَلسَّلَامُ عَلَيْكَ أَيُّهَا النَّبِيُّ$$

$$وَرَحْمَةُ اللّٰهِ وَبَرَكَاتُهُ ، اَلسَّلَامُ عَلَيْنَا وَعَلَى عِبَادِ اللّٰهِ الصَّالِحِيْنَ ،$$

17

أَشْهَدُ اَن لَّا اِلٰهَ اِلَّا اللهُ وَاَشْهَدُ اَنَّ مُحَمَّدًا عَبْدُهُ وَرَسُوْلُهُ .

[Transcription: At-ta-hiy-yaatu lillaahi was sala-waatu wat-tayyibaatu, as-salaa-mu 'alay-ka ay-yuhan na-biyyu wa-rah-matul-laahi waba-ra-kaa-tuh, as-salaa-mu 'alay-naa wa-'a-laa 'i-baa-dil-laa-his saa-li-hiin, ash-hadu allaa illaaha il-lallaahu, wa-ash-hadu an-na Muhammadan 'ab-du-hu wa-ra-su-luh.]

The most blessed greetings, the purest and most sincere inclinations unto Allah. Peace be with thee O Prophet, as well as the mercy of Allah and His blessings. Peace be with us also, and the pious servants of the Lord. I attest that there is no deity save Allah and I attest that Muhammad is His servant and Apostle.

If a salaah consists of three or four rak'ahs, when we sit after the second rak'ah only the above invocation is recited, and, at the end of the last rak'ah, durood shariif and a prayer are also added to it. The durood shariif runs as follows:

اَللّٰهُمَّ صَلِّ عَلٰى مُحَمَّدٍ وَّعَلٰى آلِ مُحَمَّدٍ كَمَا صَلَّيْتَ عَلٰى اِبْرَاهِيْمَ وَعَلٰى آلِ اِبْرَاهِيْمَ اِنَّكَ حَمِيْدٌ مَّجِيْدٌ

[Transcription: Allaa-hum-ma salli 'a-laa Muhammadiw wa-'a-laa aali Muhammadin ka-maa sal-layta 'alaa Ibraahiima wa 'alaa aali Ibraahiima innaka ha-mii-dum ma-jiid.]

O Allah, bless Muhammad and his posterity (or followers) as Thou hast blest Ibraahiim (Abraham) and his posterity (or followers); Verily, Thou art the Praiseworthy, the Majestic.

اَللّٰهُمَّ بَارِكْ عَلٰى مُحَمَّدٍ وَّعَلٰى آلِ مُحَمَّدٍ كَمَا بَارَكْتَ عَلٰى اِبْرَاهِيْمَ وَعَلٰى آلِ اِبْرَاهِيْمَ اِنَّكَ حَمِيْدٌ مَّجِيْدٌ

18

[Transcription: Allaa-humma baarik 'a-laa Muhammadiw wa-'alaa aali Muhammadin kamaa baarak-ta 'alaa Ibraahiima wa-'alaa aali Ibraahiima in-naka hamiidum majiid].

O Allah, magnify Muhammad and his posterity (or followers) as Thou hast magnified Ibraahiim (Abraham) and his posterity (or followers): Verily, Thou art the Praiseworthy, the Majestic.

Through durood shariif we invoke the favours and blessings of the Lord on the Prophet (Peace be upon him) and his family, and all those who bear a special association with him. It is, after all, through the agency of the Prophet (Peace be upon him) that the divine boons of Islaam and salaah have reached us. Allah has, therefore, charged us with the duty of praying for him, his family and his descendants, at the end of each salaah as an expression of our gratitude to him. After durood shariif it is required of us to recite the under-mentioned prayer for ourselves and with it salaah is brought to an end by turning the head, first to the right and then to the left, and wishing everyone peace and blessings of the Lord.

اَللّٰهُمَّ اِنِّيْ ظَلَمْتُ نَفْسِيْ ظُلْمًا كَثِيْرًا وَّلَا يَغْفِرُ الذُّنُوْبَ اِلَّا اَنْتَ فَاغْفِرْ لِيْ مَغْفِرَةً مِّنْ عِنْدِكَ وَارْحَمْنِيْ اِنَّكَ اَنْتَ الْغَفُوْرُ الرَّحِيْمُ .

[Transcription: Allaa-humma in-nii za-lamtu nafsii zulman kathiiraw, wa-laa yagh-firudh dhu-nuba illaa an-ta, fagh-fir lii magh-fira-tam min 'in-dika war-hamnii in-naka antal ghafuu-rur rahiim.]

O Allah, I have done my soul a great harm and no one can forgive sins except Thee; so grant me forgiveness with Thy pleasure and have pity on me. Thou art Most Forgiving, Most Merciful.

By means of this prayer we make an open confession of our sins and misdeeds and beseech Allah for His Mercy and Forgiveness. It is best for us always to consider ourselves defaulters and transgressors and make an open-hearted admission of our faults and lapses, even after performing an act of worship of the class of salaah, and repose all our hopes in Divine Compassion and Mercy. We must not allow

19

pride or vanity to come near us because of our devoutness or worshipfulness for, whatever we may do, we can never hope to acquit ourselves fully of the duty of worshipping Allah and of adoring Him and rendering to Him what is His due.

All that is necessary to know about salaah has been described in this lesson. Once again, we assert that salaah is the elixir among the various modes of worship which can transform a man into an angel, in the sphere of his deeds and morals, provided that it is offered with due concentration and feelings of reverence and humbleness.

Brothers, — we just cannot afford to take lightly the significance, worth and value of salaah.

So overpowering was the Prophet's (Peace be upon him) anxiety for his followers to remain steadfast in the matter of salaah and offer it regularly and unfailingly, that he took pains to exhort them about it, even during the last moments of his life, when it had become extremely difficult for him to speak.

Muslims who neglect salaah and do nothing to establish it and to keep it alive in their midst, should imagine for the sake of Allah, how are they going to face the august Prophet (Peace be upon him) on the Day of Reckoning, how are they going to look towards him after disregarding so shamelessly his last will and testament during their life.

Come, let us all pray now in the words of Prophet Ibraahiim (Abraham) (Peace be upon him):

رَبِّ اجْعَلْنِيْ مُقِيْمَ الصَّلٰوةِ وَمِنْ ذُرِّيَّتِيْ رَبَّنَا وَتَقَبَّلْ دُعَاءٍ ،
رَبَّنَا اغْفِرْ لِيْ وَلِوَالِدَيَّ وَلِلْمُؤْمِنِيْنَ يَوْمَ يَقُوْمُ الْحِسَابُ .

[Transcription: Rabbij 'alnii mu-qii-mas sa-laati wa-min dhur-riyyatii, rabbanaa wa-ta-qabbal du'aa, rabba-nagh-firlii wa-li-waa-li-dayya wa-lil mu-mi-niina yauma yaqu-mul hi-saab.]

20

"Oh my Lord! Make me one who establishes regular Prayer, and also (raise such) among my offsprings; Oh my Lord! And accept Thou my Prayer. Oh our Lord! cover (us) with Thy Forgiveness - me, my parents and all believers on the Day that Reckoning will be established." — Surah Ibraahiim (XIV), 40-41.

For a more detailed description of wudu, salaah etc., refer to a book on fiqh (Islaamic jurisprudence), or learn it from an 'aa-lim (learned scholar).

Lesson 3

Zakaah

AMONG THE FUNDAMENTAL TENETS of Islaam, zakaah[1] occupies a place next in importance only to belief and ṣalaah. As one would say, it is the third pillar of Islaam.

Zakaah means that a Muslim who is in possession of a certain amount of wealth, or more, is required by religion to spend one-fortieth of it at the end of every twelve months on the poor, the needy and the wayfarer, and on such items of charity and good-doing as are prescribed for it by Allah and the Prophet (Peace be upon him).

Importance

At several places in the Qur-aan, zakaah has been enjoined upon Muslims side by side with ṣalaah. While reading the Qur-aan you would have come across a number of times the command: 'Be steadfast in prayer; practise regular charity.' On several occasions it has been spoken of in the Qur-aan as a characteristic feature of Muslims that they establish prayer and practise regular charity. These two verses go to show emphatically that those who do not offer ṣalaah and fail to pay zakaah are, in fact, not Muslims, for the two basic attributes and distinguishing features of a true Muslim are not present in them.

Anyway, habitual neglect of ṣalaah, and failure to practise zakaah are, according to the Qur-aan, not the qualities of a Muslim, but of an atheist or a polytheist. About ṣalaah we have a verse in Surah Ruum of the Qur-aan which reads:

---

1. Rules governing zakaah can be found in books on Islaamic Jurisprudence or learnt directly from the 'ulama.

"Establish regular Prayer and be not ye among those who join gods with Allah." — *Surah Ruum (XXX), 31.*

And about the evasion of zakaah being the attribute of polytheists and infidels, we have it in Surah Fussilat:

"And woe to those who join gods with Allah, those who practise not regular charity, and who even deny the hereafter." — *Surah Fussilat (XLI), 6-7.*

Dreadful Chastisement

The fate that awaits those who do not pay zakaah, and the punishment that is going to be handed out to them in the hereafter, is so dreadful that the mere thought of it is enough to make one's hair stand on end. For instance, it is stated in Surah Taubah:

"And there are those who bury gold and silver and spend it not in the way of Allah; announce unto them a most grievous penalty — On the Day when heat will be produced out of that (wealth) in the fire of hell, and with it will be brand their forehead, their flanks and their backs. 'This is the (treasure) which ye buried for yourselves. Taste ye the (treasure) ye buried." — *Surah Taubah (IX), 34-35.*

In one of his ahaadiith, (traditions) the Prophet (Peace be upon him), has explained in a little more detail the purport of this surah. The hadiith (tradition) when translated into English reads:

"He who possesses gold or silver (i.e. wealth) but does not fulfil the obligations that are attached to the possession of wealth (i.e., does not pay zakaah etc.), plates of fire will be prepared for him on the Day of Judgement. These plates will be heated further in the Fire of Hell and then his forehead and his sides and back will be branded with them. The plates will be heated up again and again to brand him and this will continue throughout the Day of Judgement which will be equal to fifty thousand years in this world."

Besides it, other horrible kinds of punishment are also mentioned in the ahaadiith (traditions). May Allah save us all from them.

23

Unjust and ungrateful

People who have been blessed by Allah with wealth and prosperity are, indeed, a most unjust and ungrateful lot if they do not pay zakaah and shirk from spending their riches in His way as desired by Him. They richly deserve the punishment that is going to be meted out to them on the Day of Recompense.

Again, what is generally not realised, is that it is our own poor and indigent brothers we serve when we pay zakaah or spend our money on other acts of charity. By evading zakaah we, as such, do a great wrong to our needy and helpless brethren and play foul with their rights.

To think of it from another angle, whatever we have by way of property or wealth has, after all, been granted to us by Allah, and we are His creatures and bondsmen. He commands full control and authority over our possessions as He does over our lives. Were He to demand from us every bit of our property or our life itself, our duty, even then, would lie in placing everything before Him, quietly and without demur. It is merely His kindness and benevolence that He has called on us to give away in zakaah only one-fortieth of the wealth He has bestowed on us.

Reward

Another extraordinary favour of the Lord is that He has placed an enormous reward on zakaah and other deeds of charity, though whatever we give away is only out of the possessions and the wealth He has been pleased to bestow on us. It would have been perfectly reasonable and justified if there had been no promise of a reward from Him on these things. If He is pleased with our conduct when we spend, from the resources He has favoured us with, in zakaah and other charitable activities, as ordained by Him, and has given the assurance of a rich premium on such deeds of ours, it is solely due to

His Infinite Kindness and Mercy. States the Qur-aan:

"The parable of those who spend their substance in the Way of Allah is that of a grain of corn. It groweth seven ears and each ear hath a hundred grains. Allah giveth manifold increase to whom He pleaseth, for Allah careth for all and He knoweth all things. Those who spend their substance in the Cause of Allah, and follow not up their gifts with reminders of their generosity or with injury, - their reward is with their Lord, on them shall be no fear nor shall they grieve." — Surah Baqarah (II), 261-62.

In the above verse, three promises have been made on behalf of Allah to those who practise zakaah and spend their money in His Way through other means:

One, Allah will repay them hundred-fold in this world for what they spend;

Two, they will be rewarded bounteously in the hereafter;

Three, there will be for them neither fear nor grief on the Day of Judgement.

The noble Companions had the fullest faith in these promises. When verses extolling the spiritual merit of spending in the path of Allah and denoting what stupendous Divine Reward there was in it, were revealed to the Prophet (Peace be upon him) and the companions came to know of them from him, they were so deeply stirred that such of them as were poor and did not have the means to give away something in charity left their homes and went out in search of work and carried heavy loads on their backs so that they could earn some money to spend for the sake of Allah.

We will produce here just one hadii<u>th</u> (tradition) of the noble Prophet (Peace be upon him), revealing the significance and outstanding worth and merit of zakaah.

States the Prophet (Peace be upon him): "There are three things, whoever acquires them acquires the real joy of Faith: Firstly, to worship Allah and no one besides Him; secondly, to believe sincerely in 'Laa ilaaha illal-laah'; and, lastly, to pay the zakaah willingly on one's possessions every year."

Worldly advantages

Apart from the reward and recompense in the hereafter, numerous worldly advantages also accrue from practising zakaah regularly and spending in other divinely prescribed branches of charity. For example, a Muslim who discharges these obligations properly experiences a rare feeling of satisfaction and tranquillity in his heart, the poor do not feel jealous of his wealth — on the other hand, they wish him well, pray for his welfare and look towards him with love and admiration — the world holds him in high esteem. Everyone likes him and feels drawn towards him sympathetically — and, Allah bestows prosperity on him and multiplies his wealth.

A hadiith (tradition) of the noble Prophet (Peace be upon him) in Abu Daawuud reads:

"The mandate of Allah is: 'O Son of Adam! Go on spending the wealth I have given thee (on the poor, the needy and the destitute): I shall give thee more."

And another:

"I swear no one will become poor because of spending in the way of Allah."

May Allah endow us all with staunchest faith in the sayings of the august Prophet (Peace be upon him) and grant us the great good fortune to act on them!.

Lesson 4

Saum

AFTER BELIEF, SALAAH AND ZAKAAH, the most important duty in Islaam is saum (or fasting). The Qur-aan says:

"Oh ye who believe! fasting is prescribed to you as it was prescribed to those before you that ye may (learn) self-restraint." — *Surah Baqarah (II), 183.*

Fasting is obligatory for Muslims in the month of Ramadaan. Failure to observe the fast on any day, without a valid reason, during this month, is a great sin. We have it on the authority of the noble Prophet (Peace be upon him) that "Anyone who does not, without illness or any other valid excuse, keep fast on a single day during Ramadaan, will not succeed in making amends for it even if he were to keep fast daily throughout his life in atonement."

Recompense

During the fast, a Muslim abstains from eating and drinking and denies himself the pleasures of legitimate carnal satisfaction solely as a measure of worship, and sacrifices his lawful biological needs and urges exclusively for the sake of Allah. Allah, too, therefore, has placed a most unique reward on it. The Prophet (Peace be upon him) . is reported to have said:

"There is a fixed principle for rewarding all the good deeds of men, and every good deed will be rewarded in accordance with it. But the fast is an exception to this general principle. Allah Ta'aala commands regarding this. Since a man forgoes food and drink and crushes his passion utterly for His sake, He will recompense him directly for it."

"All the previous sins of a person are forgiven who undertakes the fasts of the month of Ramadaan with full faith and with the object of propitiating Allah and earning His reward."

27

"There are two moments of special joy for a person who fasts: One is when he breaks the fast, and this he experiences here in his earthly existence, the other will come in the hereafter when he will be presented before the Lord."

"Saum is a shield against the Fire of Hell and a strong fortress (which will protect the Believer from infernal chastisement)."

"The fast itself will plead with Allah for him who does fasting, that he had gone without the day's meals and shunned the cravings of the flesh for its sake (so he may be forgiven and rewarded to the full). Allah will accept the intercession."

"The bad odour emanating from the mouth of a person who is fasting (which is, sometimes, produced because of the empty stomach) is more pleasant in the judgement of Allah than the sweet smell of musk."

Another outstanding feature of saum, besides those given in the ahaadiith (traditions) quoted above, is that it lifts man above the level of beasts. To eat and to drink at will and to copulate whenever the urge comes, is the way of the animals. On the other extreme, to be immune from hunger and thirst and the impulsions of sex, to stay away permanently from food and drink and cohabitation, is the quality of angels. When a person fasts he rises above the animal existence and forges an affinity with angels.

Special benefit

Moreover, saum promotes piety and righteousness in man. It produces in him the ability to control his physical desires. It teaches him how to subordinate his carnal appetites and longings of the heart to the Will of Allah. It is, thus, most effective in the disciplining and evolution of the soul.

But these benefits can be derived only when a person conscientiously strives for them and pays due respect, while he is fasting, to the instructions laid down by the Prophet (Peace be upon him) in this connection. It is most necessary to leave strictly alone not only food and drink, but also all the major and minor sins. He must neither quarrel, nor utter a lie, nor engage himself in slander and back-biting. In brief, he should scrupulously avoid all sinful deeds, apparent as well as hidden, as is demanded of him in the ahaadiith (traditions). Some of the relevant ahaadiith (traditions) are:

"When any of you keep a fast, he should not speak an indecent or filthy word or engage in a noisy scene, and were anyone to quarrel with him and call him names, he should simply say, 'I am keeping fast (therefore, I cannot pay you back in the same coin)'."

"Allah has no need for him to go without food and drink who cannot shun evil and falsehood even during a fast."

"Many are there among you who fast and yet gain nothing from it except hunger and thirst."

In sum, fast can lead to the promotion of virtues of piety and righteousness and impart the moral strength needed to control and discipline the sensual appetites when, together with abstention from food and drink, all the major and minor transgressions of the law of Allah are, also, zealously avoided while fasting, more specially the use of foul and filthy language, falsehood, slander and back-biting. If fasts are observed in the right spirit, and with proper care and solicitude, the benefits indicated above can positively be obtained from them.

Lesson 5

Hajj

THE LAST FUNDAMENTAL DUTIES in Islaam is the hajj (or pilgrimage). Laying it down as an essential religious obligation of Muslims, the Qur-aan says:

"Pilgrimage thereto is a duty men owe to Allah - those who can afford the journey, but if any deny faith Allah stands not in need of any of His creatures." — Surah Aali 'Imraan (III), 97.

In this verse while the hajj has been declared obligatory it has been made clear that it is applicable only to those who possess the means and material resources to undertake it. But care has been taken, in the last part of it, to warn that if Muslims whom Allah has blessed with the necessary means to perform the pilgrimage still fail to carry out the duty through sheer ingratitude (as is common among the wealthy classes these days) then Allah does not stand in need of their pilgrimage. The Almighty, definitely, is not going to lose anything by their not performing the hajj; the loss will be entirely theirs. They will forfeit His good graces; they will deprive themselves of His benevolence; and Allah-forbid, a most lamentable fate will be awaiting them in the hereafter. The Prophet (Peace be upon him) is reported to have gone as far as to say:

"A person whom Allah has given enough to perform the hajj, if he still fails to do so, then it does not matter at all whether he dies a Jew or a Christian."

Brothers, — if there is any regard in our hearts for Islaam, if we can boast of the least attachment to Allah and the Prophet (Peace be upon him), none of us who can afford to make the journey should remain without performing the hajj after we know this tradition.

30

Spiritual merit

The importance of the hajj and the spiritual meritoriousness of those who perform it, have been emphasised in a number of ahaadiith (traditions). We will reproduce a few of them here.

"Those who make pilgrimage for the hajj or 'umrah, they are the guests of Allah: Their petitions, if they make any to the Lord, will be granted, and if they seek deliverance from sins, their sins will be forgiven."

"He who performs the hajj and commits no wicked or sinful deed during it and does not disobey Allah, he will return from it as pure and guiltless as he was at the time of his birth."

"The reward for a pure and untainted hajj is Paradise itself and nothing short of it."

Immediate gains

The remission of sins and the enjoyment of the supreme blissfulness of Paradise as a result of the spiritual auspiciousness of the hajj will, In-Sha-Allah, surely be granted to the faithful in full measure in the life to come, but the exquisite thrill and the sublime joy one experiences, the soul-stirring sensation of delight and wonderment one feels, on seeing that choicest seat of Divine Splendour — the Ka'bah — and on visiting those special places in Makkah where the memories of Prophet Ibraahiim (Abraham) (Peace be upon him) and of our own Prophet (Peace be upon him) are still alive, are, also, things of the celestial world on the earth. Then the pilgrimage to the Prophet's (Peace be upon him) mausoleum at Madiinah, the offering of salaah in his own masjid (mosque), the addressing of the salutation and the blessing to him directly, the aimless

31

wanderings in the streets and in the wilderness of that blessed city, the breathing in of its air and the fragrance which always seems to be filling its atmosphere, the ethereal joy of his remembrance bursting upon one, sometimes in laughter and sometimes in tears, — all these things — provided, of course, that one is blessed enough to feel them — are the immediate rewards a pilgrim gets when he betakes himself to the holy cities of Makkah and Madiinah.

Five pillars of Islaam

The five, fundamental teachings of Islaam we have discussed so far — the kalimah, salaah, zakaah, saum and hajj — are known as the Five Pillars of the Faith.

A well-known hadiith (tradition) on the holy Prophet (Peace be upon him) tells us that:

"The foundation of Islaam rests of five things:

i.   The affirmation of 'Laa ilaaha illal-laah.'
ii. The establishment of salaah.
iii. The payment of zakaah.
iv. The observance of saum in the month of Ramadaan.
v.   The performance of hajj by those who can afford to make the pilgrimage."

When these five items are spoken of as the 'Pillars of Islaam', it means these duties are capable of producing in us the ability to fulfil our other religious obligations as well. Here we have dwelt only on their importance and the intrinsic spiritual virtue that underlies them. Detailed rules and principles governing them can be learnt from reliable books on Islaamic Jurisprudence or directly from a Muslim theologian.

Lesson 6

Piety

PIETY FORMS PART OF THE BASIC essentials of Islaam. It means to observe the Divine Commandments, conscientiously and scrupulously, and to avoid all forbidden, wicked and shameful things, believing wholly and firmly in the great Requital of the Last Day, and fearing Allah and His wrath and punishment as a burnt child is supposed to dread the fire. In other words, it demands of us, on the one hand, to carry out, thoroughly and well, the duties prescribed by the Almighty and fulfil zealously the rights of men who have a claim on us according to the Divine Law, and, on the other, to refrain strictly from doing anything that has been prohibited to us by Him. It calls on us to make the fear of Allah our constant companion. Both in the Qur-aan and the ahaadiith (traditions) a very great emphasis has been laid on piety and righteousness, and it has been urged upon us most forcefully and persistently to cultivate it in ourselves. Some of the relevant verses of the Qur-aan are:

"O ye who believe! fear Allah as He should be feared, and die not except in a state of Islaam." — Surah Aaali 'Imraan (III), 102.

"So fear Allah as much as you can; listen and obey." — Surah Taghaa-bun (LXIV), 16.

"O ye who believe! fear Allah and let every soul look to what (provisions) he has sent forth for the morrow. Ye, fear Allah; for Allah is well acquainted with (all) that ye do." — Surah Hashr (LIX), 18.

The Qur-aanic verses, further, reveal that there is a great favour of the Lord even in this world on those who fear Allah and practise piety and righteousness. Allah shows special munificence to them and makes His help available to them in a thousand ways:

"And for those who fear Allah, He (ever) prepares a way out, and He provides for him from (sources) he never could imagine." — Surah Talaaq (LXV), 2-3.

33

The Qur-aan also tells that those who lead a life of piety and righteousness become the 'Friends of Allah', and, then, for them there is neither fear nor shall they ever grieve.

"Behold! verily on the Friends of Allah there is no fear nor shall they grieve, those who believe and (constantly) guard against evil; for them are Glad Tidings, in the life of the present and the hereafter." — Surah Yuunus (X), 62-64.

Some of the wonderful boons and blessings that await the pious and the righteous in the hereafter have been revealed briefly in the following verses:

"Say: 'Shall I give you glad tidings of things far better that those? For the righteous are Gardens in nearness to their Lord, with rivers flowing beneath, therein is their eternal home with companions (pure and holy), and the good pleasure of Allah. For in Allah's sight are (all) His servants'." — Surah Aaali 'Imraan (III), 15.

"And, verily, for the righteous, is a beautiful place of (final) Return. Gardens of Eternity whose doors will ever be opened to them; therein will they recline (at ease); therein can they call (at pleasure) for fruit in abundance and (delicious) drink, and besides them will be chaste women restraining their glances, (companions) of equal age. Such is the promise made to you for the Day of Account! Truly, such will be Our Bounty (to you). It will never fail." — Surah Ṣaad (XXXVIII), 49-54.

In the Qur-aan, again, men of piety are given the very special tidings of a place of exceptional nearness to Allah in the hereafter:

"As to the righteous, they will be in the midst of Gardens and Rivers, in an Assembly of Truth in the presence of a Sovereign Omnipotent." — Surah Qamar (LIV) 54-55.

The sole criterion of honour and superiority with Allah is piety.

"Verily, the most honoured of you in the sight of Allah is (he who is) the most righteous of you." — Surah Ḥuju-raat (XLIX), 13.

Similarly, it has been declared by the Prophet (Peace be upon him) in one of his aḥaadiith (traditions) that:

"Nearest and dearest to me are those who possess the virtue of piety, no matter what race or nationality they belong to or which country they live in."

Piety (i.e., fear of Allah and an over-powering anxiety for the hereafter) is the root of all virtue. It is the measure of goodness. We will be as good and noble and as free from that which is base and corrupt as there is piety in us. *

Another of the noble Prophet's (Peace be upon him) ahaadiith (traditions) reads:

"A noble Companion once said to the Prophet (Peace be upon him), 'Sir, I have heard so many of your valuable sayings that I fear I may not be able to remember them all. So I request you for a comprehensive advice which may suffice for me always.' The Prophet (Peace be upon him) replied, 'Fear Allah in proportion to your knowledge and make that fear and piety the guiding principles of your life'."

And, yet another:

"He who has fear will set out early and he who will set out early will reach the destination in time."

The fortunate and the successful, indeed, are those who fear Allah and prepare for the life to come.

Even a single tear shed out of fear of Allah and of His anger and punishment carries a great value in His eyes.

"There are two drops", says the Prophet (Peace be upon him), "and two marks, than which nothing is more precious to Allah. Of the two drops so exceedingly dear to Him, one is the tear that may have fallen from the eyes of anyone out of His fear, and the other is the drop of blood that is shed in His path. Similarly, of the two marks one is the mark sustained in the path of Allah (i.e., the scar left behind by a wound sustained in jihaad), and the other is the mark which may have developed as a result of the carrying out of religious

35

obligation (as for example, the marks one often sees on the forehead and knees of those who offer salaah regularly)."

We will take up one more hadiith (tradition) of the Prophet (Peace be upon him). It says:

"Never can he go to Hell who weeps in the fear of Allah."

The sum and substance of the entire discussion is that it is great, beyond doubt, to be blessed with true fear of Allah and a genuine solicitude for the hereafter. It can literally revolutionize one's whole existence.

Brothers, — know it thoroughly and well that one who is Allah-fearing in this transitory world will have absolutely nothing to worry in the hereafter. He will have neither fear nor anxiety. He will dwell in eternal peace, comfort and happiness, by the grace of Allah. On the contrary, he who is not Allah-fearing and shows no concern for the afterlife and refuses to look beyond the pleasures of material existence, for him there will be a terrible anguish and distress in the life to come. For thousands of years he will be shedding tears of blood.

The surest way to develop piety, i.e., Allah-fearingness and solicitude for the hereafter, is to avail oneself of the company of the devout servants of the Lord who fear Him and obey His commands honestly. Then there are good and reliable religious books which should be read regularly, and, if a person is illiterate, he should have them read out to him by others. Lastly, it is advisable to meditate in solitude on death and on the rewards one is going to get from Allah for one's good and virtuous deeds, and punishment that is going to be awarded by Him for one's sins and transgressions against the Divine Law. One should dwell mentally on one's state and visualise what is going to pass in the grave, what will one's condition be when men will be raised up again on the Last Day and brought before Allah? What will one do when the balance sheet of one's conduct on earth will be unrolled? Where will one, then, hide one's face?

Lesson 7

Honesty in monetary dealings

UPRIGHTNESS AND HONESTY in monetary dealings forms a vital part of the fundamental teachings of Islaam.

The Qur-aan as well as the ahaadiith (traditions) of the Prophet (Peace be upon him) are emphatic that a true Muslim is he who is honest and upright in his business and other monetary transactions; keeps his word and fulfils his promises; shuns fraud and avoids deceit; encroaches not upon the rights of others; abstains from wrongful litigation; does not give false evidence; and abstains from making dishonest money as from usury and graft. Whoever is not free from these vices is, according to the Qur-aan and the ahaadiith (traditions), not a true Believer but a renegade and a worthless transgressor.

We now proceed to examine some of the relevant Qur-aanic verses and ahaadiith (traditions). A short verse of the Qur-aan says:

"O ye who believe! eat not up each other's property by unfair and dishonest means." — Surah Nisaa (IV), 29.

The verse forbids Muslims against all unclean and corrupt means of making money, such as, dishonest trading, embezzlement, gambling, speculation and bribery. Then there are verses in which these hateful practices are dealt with one by one.

For instance, a severe warning is given in the following verse to traders who cheat in weighing:

"Woe to those that deal in fraud, those who, when they have to receive by measure from men, exact full measure, but when they have to give by measure or weight to men, give less than due. Do they not think that they will be called to account on a Mighty Day when (all) mankind will stand before the Lord of the Worlds." — Surah Mu-taffifiin (LXXXIII), 1-6.

In the same way, the undermentioned verse exhorts Muslims to be very particular about their trusts and about other people's rights.

"Allah doth command you to render back your trusts to those to whom they are due." — Surah Nisaa (IV), 58.

At two places in the Qur-aan (Surah Mu-minuun and Ma'aarij) a chief distinguishing feature of Muslims is said to be that they are:

"Those who faithfully observe their trusts and their covenants." — Surah Mu-minuun (XXIII), 8.

The Prophet (Peace be upon him) often used to say in his sermons:

"Remember, there is no Faith in him who is not trustworthy: there is no place for him in religion who cares not for his pledged word or promise."

"Another hadiith (tradition) says: 'The signs of a hypocrite are three: When he speaks, he is false; when he promises, he fails; and when he is trusted, he plays false'."

Condemning those who cheat in business, the sacred Prophet (Peace be upon him) has said, "He who cheats is not of us. Deceitfulness and fraud are things that lead one to Hell."

"The Prophet (Peace be upon him) of Allah once came upon a heap of corn in the market of Madiinah and thrust his hand into it. His fingers felt damp. On being asked, the trader replied that rain had fallen upon it. The Prophet (Peace be upon him) observed, 'Why did you not, then, keep (the wet portion of) it above the dry corn so that men may see it? He who deceives is not one of us'."

Thus, traders who deceive by showing to customers a false sample or by concealing from them the defects of the article they offer for sale, are not true Muslims in the judgement of the noble Prophet (Peace be upon him), and, Allah-forbid, they are going to end up in Hell. Another hadiith (tradition) says: "The seller must explain to the buyer the defects, if any, in the quality of the article offered for sale. Should this not be done, the seller will permanently be caught in the wrath of Allah (according to another narrator the exact words are, he will always be cursed by the angels').''

In short, all manner of deceit and dishonesty in business is prohibited in Islaam. It has been proclaimed to be an act worthy of unqualified condemnation. The noble Prophet (Peace be upon him) has expressed his strong dislike for those who do so. He has said that he will have nothing to do with them. They do not belong to him.

Likewise, bribery and usury, although they might be practised by mutual consent and agreement, are totally disallowed to Muslims and those who are guilty of them have been condemned squarely in the hadiith (tradition). A well-known hadiith on usury reads:

''The curse of Allah rests on him who offers loan on usurious terms, and on him who receives, and on those who are witnesses to the transaction, and on the writer who writes the deed thereof.''

As for bribery, a hadiith (tradition) states, ''The Prophet (Peace be upon him) cursed the giver and taker of bribes.''

A hadiith (tradition) goes even to the extent of saying that a person made a recommendation for anyone in a just matter and the gratified party gave him something as a gift (in return for it) and he accepted it, then he committed a grave error (meaning that it, too, is a form of bribery).

Worse still is the usurpation of another's property by force or fraud or dishonest litigation. We have it on the authority of the Prophet (Peace be upon him) that:

''Whoever occupies land belonging to another unjustly will be sunk into the ground along with that plot of land on the Doomsday till he reaches the lowest layer of the earth.''

''He who acquires the property of a Muslim unjustly by taking a false oath (before an officer) is debarred by Allah from entering Paradise and the Fire of Hell is made inevitable for him.'' On hearing it, a Companion is reported to have asked, ''Even if it be a minor

39

thing?" The Prophet (Peace be upon him) is said to have replied, "Yes, even if it be a twig of pilo (a plant which grows wild and its twigs are used for cleaning the teeth)."

The Prophet (Peace be upon him), again, is reported to have warned a person who was very fond of entering into litigation with others in these strong words, "Remember, he who will obtain the property of another by swearing a false oath will appear as a leper before Allah (on the Day of Judgement)."

And again:

"Whoever laid his claim on a thing that was not his is not of us. He will do well to reserve a place for himself in Hell."

It is narrated that one day, after the morning prayers, the noble Prophet (Peace be upon him) stood up and said thrice with great feeling that: "Perjury has been made the equivalent of polytheism."

Ill-gotten wealth

Money or property which is acquired through unfair means, as we have just indicated, is positively unclean and unlawful and anyone who makes use of it and spends it on his needs does himself a great harm. As the sacred Prophet (Peace be upon him) has warned, his prayers will not find acceptance with Allah; his supplications will not be answered, his petitions will not be granted; and in case he does good deeds they will avail him nothing. In the hereafter, there will be no share for him in the special favours and good graces of the Lord.

A hadiith (tradition) says: "If a person earns or acquires anything through dishonest means, and, then, gives away a part of it in charity, his act of charity will not be accepted, and if he will spend from it on his needs there will be no auspiciousness or real prosperity in it, and should he leave it behind to his descendants, on his death, it will serve for him as Hell's provision. Believe it, Allah does not erase evil with evil (i.e., charity and almsgiving from ill-gotten gains can never lead to salvation). One impurity cannot remove another; it cannot make it pure."

And, another:

"Allah is pure Himself and He accepts only offerings that are pure."

The Prophet (Peace be upon him), at the end of the hadiith (tradition), also narrated the story of a man, "Who undertakes a long and tedious journey (to supplicate to Allah at a haloed place) and arrives (at his destination) in such a state that his hair is dishevelled and his body is covered from head to foot with dust. He throws up his hands towards the heavens and cries out, 'O Lord! O my Preserver!' but his sustenance is of the impure and he has been brought up on what is polluted; how can his prayer be granted when such is the case?' "

The above amply demonstrates that when a person draws his livelihood from impure means his prayers no longer remain worthy of being answered. Yet another hadiith (tradition) of the noble Prophet (Peace be upon him) reads:

"If a person buys a cloth for ten dirhams[1] and of them one dirham is tainted (i.e., it has been earned dishonestly), none of his salaah will be accepted by Allah as long as he wears it."

And, here is one more:

"The flesh gathered on one's body by means of unclean income deserves to be thrown into the Fire."

Brothers, — if we have the tiniest spark of Faith left in our bosom we must make up our minds, once for all, after hearing of the ahaadiith (traditions), that whatever poverty and hardship we may

---

1. Dirham is said to be an unstamped piece of silver which was current in Arabia of those days as a coin. Later it was altered into a round form and stamped. Its value is uncertain. — Translator.

have to endure in the world, we will never care to make a single cent from unclean and dishonest sources and will always content ourselves with what we earn through honest and lawful means.

Clean earning and honest trade

Just as Islaam has condemned all unclean and unlawful means of making money as wicked and sinful and denouncing all profits derived from them as filthy and devilish, in the same way it has proclaimed great virtue in seeking one's livelihood honestly and in engaging oneself cleanly in trade or profession. The Prophet (Peace be upon him) has said:

"To earn a clean living is also a duty next only to the prescribed duties of the Faith."

"The cleanest food is that which has been earned by the labour of one's hand. Indeed, Prophet Daawuud (David) (Peace be upon him) used to work with his own hands for the food he ate."

"The trader who plies his trade cleanly and honestly will rise in the hereafter in the company of Prophets, saints and martyrs."

Kindness and compassion in monetary dealings

Islaam has laid great stress on honesty and truthfulness in trade and other monetary dealings and described profound virtue and excellence in it. It has declared it to be a means of gaining nearness unto Allah. Islaam, likewise, enjoins upon us to be kind and avoid harshness and severity in our monetary transactions and has promised great spiritual advantage in it also. We will reproduce two of the Prophet's (Peace be upon him) ahaadiith (traditions) here:

"Blessings of Allah be on him who is mild and gentle in business transactions and in the realisation of dues."

"Allah will protect him from the agonies of the Day of Judgement who allows respite to a poor and indigent servant of His in the payment of his debt or writes off the debt (altogether or a part of it)."

These a_haadii_th (traditions) are meant for merchants and other wealthy men from whom people borrow money in the hour of their need. As for the borrowers, the Prophet (Peace be upon him) used to urge them to do their best to pay back their debts quickly, lest they die in a state of indebtedness with the claim of anyone lying unsettled on their heads. How strict the Prophet (Peace be upon him) was in this regard can be imagined from the following a_haadii_th (traditions):

"If a person is killed in the path of Allah then all his sins will be forgiven (by virtue of martyrdom). But if he owes anyone anything, even martyrdom will not secure his release from it."

"By the Lord in whose power lies the life of Mu_hammad, if a person falls a martyr in the path of Allah and returns to life, and is killed again in the path of Allah, and returns to life only to be killed once more in the cause of Allah, and there is still a debt outstanding against him, (until it is settled) even he will not be able to enter Paradise."

These two a_haadii_th (traditions) are quite sufficient to show what great importance Islaam attaches to monetary affairs and the rights of men. May Allah grant us the wisdom to understand their delicateness and significance and make it our constant endeavour to assure that the claims of no one are left unpaid by us!

Lesson 8

Social conduct and mutual relations

SOCIAL CONDUCT, GOOD MANNERS and respect for the rights of each other, again, form an important part of Islaamic teachings. One can become a good and true Muslim only when one also observes faithfully the social code of Islaam, by which we mean the rules and regulations governing the modes and manners of behaviour between man and man and between man and society, as laid down by it. For instance, what should the attitude of parents be towards their children and of children towards their parents? What sort of conduct should prevail between brothers and between brothers and sisters? How should husband and wife live together? How are we to treat those who are older than ourselves and those that are younger? What are the rights of neighbours on us? How should the rich behave towards the poor and the poor towards the rich? What mode of relationship should one obtain between master and servant? And, so forth. Islaam has provided us with a most precise and complete guidance on how we are to fulfil our social responsibilities and act in our dealings and relationships with all those individuals and groups with whom we come into contact, one way or the other, in the different walks of our daily life, and this is what we are going to discuss in the present chapter.

Rights of parents

The most primary relationship in this world exists between man and his parents. In Islaam the rights of parents have been described as next only to the rights of Allah. To quote from the Qur-aan:

"The Lord has ordained that ye worship none but Him; and to show kindness to your parents whether one or both of them attain to old age with thee; and say not to them Fie!" Neither reproach them; but speak to them both with respectful speech; and defer humbly to them out of tenderness; and say,

44

"Lord! have compassion on them both, even as they reared me when I was little." — Surah Israa [Banii Israa-eel] (XVII), 23-24.

Another verse of the Truthful Book goes on to tell that, should the parents of a person be polytheists and want him also to follow their faith, he ought to decline to obey them, but even then he should continue to treat them well and to behave towards them with respect. The exact words of the verse are:

"But if they strive to make thee join in worship with Me, things of which thou hast no knowledge, obey them not; yet bear them company in this life with justice (and consideration)." — Surah Luqmaan (XXXI), 15.

Besides the Qur-aan, and in the ahaadiith (traditions), also, a very great stress has been laid on rendering full devotion and obedience to one's parents. To disobey one's parents, to ignore their feelings, or to disregard their comfort and happiness in any other way, has been characterised by the Prophet (Peace be upon him) as a grievous sin. Take these ahaadiith (traditions), for example:

"In the pleasure of parents lies the pleasure of Allah, and in their displeasure, the displeasure of Allah."

"Once a person enquired from the Prophet (Peace be upon him), 'What are the rights of parents?' The Prophet (Peace be upon him) replied, 'Parents are the Heaven and Hell of their children (meaning, salvation and Paradise could be gained by serving one's parents well while disobedience to and ill-treatment of them could lead one to Hell)'."

"The Prophet (Peace be upon him) once observed, 'Every time a dutiful son or daughter looks with affection and respect towards his or her father or mother, Allah writes against his or her name the reward of an approved hajj.' Upon this, some of the Companions enquired, 'Our Master! Suppose a person does so a hundred times each day, will he, even then, be given the reward of an approved hajj for every glance he casts?' 'Yes', the Prophet (Peace be upon him) replied, 'Allah is Most Great, Most Pure (meaning that the bounty of the Lord is boundless)'."

45

"Heaven lies under the feet of parents."

"The Prophet (Peace be upon him) once said to the Companions that the most mortal sins in the world are three: 'To associate anyone with Allah, to disobey parents, and to give false evidence'."

Again, "There are three types of men towards whom Allah will not look with mercy on the Day of Judgement and one of them are those who disobey their parents."

Rights of children

Islaam has laid an equal stress on the rights of children on parents also. We will leave out here the responsibility of parents to feed and clothe their children, since there is found in them an instinctive awareness of it and they carry it out normally and in a natural way.

The rights of our children, about which we are generally careless and neglectful, are those concerning their moral and religious education and upbringing. Islaam has made it binding on us, as a matter of duty, that we bring up our wards and children in such a way that they do not have to make their way to Hell after death. We are required to be extremely careful in this respect. Says the Qur-aan:

"O ye who believe! save yourselves and your families from the Fire of Hell."
— *Surah Tahriim (LXVI), 6.*

The Prophet (Peace be upon him) has, in a hadiith (tradition), stressed the need of giving proper training to children in these words:

"No better gift can there be from a father to his children than bringing them up properly."

Some parents are more fond of their sons than daughters. They take a great interest in the upbringing of their male offspring, while the welfare and training of female ones is generally neglected. Daughters are, sometimes, considered to be a burden. For this reason,

46

Islaam has devoted particular attention to the proper upbringing of girls and extolled it as an act of great virtue. The august Prophet (Peace be upon him) has said:

"Anyone who has a daughter or a sister and he treats her well and looks after her welfare and training carefully, and marries her at the right place, Allah will reward him with Paradise."

Mutual rights between husband and wife

Conjugal relationship occupies a place of outstanding importance in the economy of human affairs. It is a most strong and intimate tie that binds husband and wife into a lifelong partnership. Islaam, therefore, has furnished a complete guidance in respect of it as well. In a nutshell; Islaam demands from wives to be scrupulously faithful to their husbands and to remain their best friends and true well-wishers and never to betray their trusts. The Qur-aan declares:

"Therefore, the righteous women are obedient, and guard (in the husband's) absence." — Surah Nisaa (IV), 34.

And from husbands, it requires that they should give of their love ungrudgingly to their wives, maintain them as best as they can within their means and leave nothing to be desired by way of emotional contentment. Says, again, the Qur-aan:

"Live with your wives on a footing of kindness and equity." — Surah Nisaa (IV), 19.

In keeping with these teachings of the Qur-aan, the Prophet (Peace be upon him) used to attach profound importance to the harmony of married life among Muslims. He used to urge upon Muslim husbands and wives to keep each other happy and to attend to each other's needs and interests with loving care. Some of his ahaadiith (traditions) in this connection read:

47

"If a man calls his wife to him and the wife refuses and he stays annoyed with her during the night, the angels will not cease to curse her name till daybreak."

"The woman who dies in such a state that her husband is pleased with her shall go to Heaven."

"By the Lord in whose power lies the life of Muḥammad, no woman can fulfil the rights of Allah who does not fulfil the rights of her husband."

"I charge you to be kind to your wives. Remember this advice of mine. See, they are subordinate to you and in your power."

"Good among you are those who are good to their wives."

"He is the most perfect believer (in Allah) who is perfect in his manners and most affectionate towards his wife and children."

Rights of relatives

Besides our parents and children and husbands or wives, there also exists a special tie of kinship between us and our relatives. Islaam has paid due attention to this aspect of our social existence, too, and evolved certain rights and duties in respect of it. Thus, in the Qur-aan we are told to be kind to our kinsmen, and one who disregards and pays no heed to the bonds of kinship has been condemned as a transgressor and sinner of the worst order.

"The Prophet (Peace be upon him) once said, 'He who violates the rights of kinsmen and shows no respect for the bonds of kinship in his conduct shall not go to Heaven'."

"In this connection a special advice of the Prophet (Peace be upon him) is that if a relative violates the ties of relationship with regard to us even then we should continue to fulfil, on our part, the obligations we have towards him. The exact words of the noble Prophet (Peace be upon him) are, 'If a near relative treats you indifferently and ignores the bond of relationship do not turn your back on him but keep on discharging, on your part, the obligations of relationship towards him'."

Rights of the old on the young and of the young on the old

It is a general principle of Islaamic social behaviour that everyone should respect his elders and carry himself with due deference in their presence. In the same way, those who are older are required to treat those who are younger to them with kindness and affection, even if there be no relationship between them.

"Said the Prophet (Peace be upon him): 'He is not of us who is not affectionate to those who are younger than himself and respectful to those who are older'."

"For the young man who will honour an old man because of his age, Allah will appoint men who will honour him in his old age."

Rights of neighbours

Apart from relatives, there exists a permanent association also between a man and his neighbours. In Islaam full attention has, accordingly, been paid to it and definite instructions have been provided for our guidance in this behalf as well. The Qur-aan calls upon us to be good and courteous in our behaviour towards our neighbours in the same way as it has commanded us to maintain the best of conduct towards our parents, brothers and sisters and towards other near relatives:

"Neighbours who are near, neighbours who are strangers, the companions by your side." — Surah Nisaa (IV), 36.

49

Three categories of neighbours have been spoken of in this verse and it is expected of us to maintain cordial relations with all of them.

The phrase 'Neighbours who are near' denotes neighbours who may also happen to be our relatives; 'Neighbours who are strangers' denotes those with whom we have no family ties, and 'Companions by our side' means persons with whom we come into contact temporarily in the course of our daily activities, like a casual acquaintance, an intimate friend, a fellow traveller, a classmate and colleague, whatever their religious denomination. Islaam reminds us that we have an obligation to be friendly and sympathetic towards all the three categories of neighbours.

Says the august Prophet (Peace be upon him):

"He who believes in Allah and the Day of Recompense will never harm his neighbour."

"He is not a Muslim who eats his fill and lets his neighbour go hungry."

"It is narrated that the Apostle of Allah once emphatically exclaimed, 'He is not a believer in Allah', The question was asked, 'O Apostle of Allah! Who is not a believer in Allah?' The Prophet (Peace be upon him) observed, 'Whose neighbour does not feel secure on his account'."

Yet another hadiith (tradition) reads:

"He shall not go to Heaven from whose mischief his neighbours do not feel secure."

"It is reported that once a Companion said to the Prophet (Peace be upon him), 'Sir, there is a woman about whom it is said that she offers a great deal of prayers, observes a great deal of fasts and does a great deal of charity, but she also causes a great deal of trouble to her neighbours owing to the sharpness of her tongue.' The noble Prophet (Peace be upon him) observed, 'She will go to Hell.' The Companion then said, 'O Apostle of Allah! There is another woman about whom it is said that she engages herself little in prayers, fasting and charity (that is, she observes the supererogatory prayers, fasts and charity less than the first woman) but never offends her neighbours by her tongue.' The august Prophet (Peace be upon him) observed, 'She will be in Heaven'."

Brothers, — such are the rights of neighbours in Islaam. Alas, how heedless have we now grown of them!

Rights of the weak and poor

So far we have dealt with the rights of men with whom we have an intimate personal connection of some kind, whether of family or neighbourhood or business or friendship. In addition to these, Islaam has conferred certain special rights on the weaker and the poorer sections of the society, and on every kind of a needy person. It has been made the duty of all well-to-do people to look after their well-being and serve them in whatever way they can. The more prosperous among Muslims should realise that their less fortunate brethren, too, have a share in their wealth and other capabilities. The Qur-aan has enjoined at a number of places that the needs of the orphans, the weak and the indigent and other needy and destitute persons should be taken care of, the hungry should be fed, the ill-clad should be clothed, and so on.

"It is narrated that once the Prophet (Peace be upon him) joined two of his fingers and showing them to the Companions said, 'He who supports an orphan shall be as close to me in Heaven as these fingers are to each other'."

"He who endeavours to relieve the widow, the depressed and the needy, is as one who strives in the service of Allah, and, in divine reward, he is as one who permanently fasts during the day and spends one's nights in prayers."

"Feed the hungry, visit the sick and free the captives."

"Help the distressed and be a guide to those who have lost their way."

51

No distinction has been drawn in the above ahaadiith (traditions) of the Prophet (Peace be upon him) between a Muslim and a non-Muslim. All poor and needy persons have a claim on us no matter to what religion they belong. We cannot withhold our helping hand from anyone on the ground that he is not a co-religionist. In some ahaadiith (traditions), the Prophet (Peace be upon him) has exhorted us to show kindness also to animals and promised a great reward to those who take pity on these dumb creatures of the Lord.

Islaam, truly, is a blessing to the entire universe and the whole of creation, and our guide and master, the Prophet Muhammad (Peace be upon him), "A mercy to the worlds." The pity is that we ourselves have wandered away from his teachings. Would to Allah that we, too, became a mercy to the whole world by becoming true Muslims!

Rights of Muslims on each other

Further, there is a special claim of Muslims on each other which flows out of the common bond of Islaam.

Says the Prophet (Peace be upon him):

"Every Muslim is a Muslim's brother. He should neither harm him himself nor leave him alone (when someone else does so but try his best to help him and to protect him). Whoever among you will fulfil the need of his brother, Allah will take it upon Himself to fulfil his needs, and a Muslim who will remove the distress of a Muslim brother will, in return, find a distress of his removed by Allah on the Day of Requital, and anyone who will hide the shame of a Muslim, his sins will be hidden by Allah on the Last Day."

"Do not bear a grudge or enmity against each other, do not be jealous of each other, and do not indulge in backbiting."

"Live like brothers and the servants of One Allah. It is not allowed to a Muslim to cease to be on talking terms with another Muslim for more than three days."

52

"The life, honour and property of a Muslim are sacred for another."

We will now close the present discussion on social relations and mutual rights and duties with the following ḥadiith (tradition) which alone is enough to fill our hearts with fear. "The Prophet (Peace be upon him) is reported one day, to have put the question to the Companions. 'Who is a pauper?' The Companions replied, 'Our master! A pauper is a person who is without a cent of his own.' The Prophet (Peace be upon him) said, 'No. A pauper among us is a man who will appear on the Day of Recompense with a large stock of prayers, fasting and almsgiving but in the world he would have abused someone, slandered someone, beaten someone and cheated and transgressed against someone. When he will be made to stand at the Place of Reckoning, those against whom he would have been guilty of these transgressions, will come forward and they will be given from his good deeds what will be due to them till all the fund of his good deeds will be exhausted, and, then, the sins of the aggrieved parties will be forced down upon him and, he will, ultimately, be thrown into Hell'."

Brothers, — ponder over this ḥadiith (tradition) and think how utterly ruinous and disastrous it is for us to encroach upon the rights of others and indulge in backbiting, slander or abuse. If you have transgressed against anyone or usurped his rights, make amends for it in your lifetime, pay back to him what may be his due or seek his forgiveness, and resolve sincerely to be careful in future, otherwise it is going to cost you very dear in the life to come.

Lesson 9

Good manners and noble qualities

GOOD MANNERS AND NOBLE QUALITIES of mind and character enjoy a place of crucial importance in the structure of Islaamic teachings. Moral evolution and upliftment was one of the main objects for which the sacred Prophet (Peace be upon him) was sent. The Prophet (Peace be upon him) himself has said:

"I have been sent down by Allah to teach moral virtues and to evolve them to highest perfection."

Importance

An idea of the enormous importance Islaam attaches to the cultivation of good manners and noble moral qualities can be obtained from the undermentioned a<u>h</u>aadii<u>th</u> (traditions) of the Prophet (Peace be upon him):

"The best of you are those who possess the best of manners."

"On the Day of Recompense nearest to me will be one who displays in one's daily life the best of manners."

"On the Day of Reckoning the most weighty item in the 'Balance of Deeds' will be good manners."

"Once a Companion asked the Prophet (Peace be upon him), 'What is there that takes a Muslim to Paradise?' The Prophet (Peace be upon him) replied, 'Fear of Allah and good manners'."

"The Prophet (Peace be upon him), again, is reported to have said, 'A Muslim with good manners and good moral disposition gets the same reward as he who fasts (permanently) during the day and spends his nights in prayer'."

The last ḥadiith (tradition) tells that a Believer who possesses good manners and carries out scrupulously the moral duties imposed on him by Allah, but does not engage himself much in supererogatory fasts and prayers, attains the degree of excellence of the man who stands up in prayer all night and fasts all day long.

The curse of bad manners

We have been warned by the august Prophet (Peace be upon him) in an equally forceful manner against the curse of bad manners. He has said:

"A man with bad manners and a bad moral conduct shall not enter Paradise."

"No sin is more detestable to Allah than bad manners."

Some more important virtues

In the Qur-aan and the aḥaadiith (traditions) we are taught to cultivate all good and noble moral and social qualities and to avoid everything that is mean or wicked, here we will take up only such virtues that are more important and without which no one can hope to be a good Muslim and a truthful Believer.

Truthfulness

Truthfulness is a matter of such supreme consequence in Islaam that, in addition to speaking the truth always, a Muslim is exhorted, also, to keep company only with those that are truthful. The Qur-aan states:

"O ye who believe! fear Allah and be only with those who are true (in word and deed)." — Surah Taubah (IX), 119.

Says the Prophet (Peace be upon him):

"He who wishes to love Allah and His Apostle, or wishes Allah and His Apostle to love him, must take care to speak nothing but the truth whenever he speaks."

"Speak the truth even if you see your ruin or death in it, for surely, salvation and life lie alone in truth, and avoid falsehood even if it may hold out to you the promise of success and salvation, for the end of falsehood is nothing but failure and frustration."

"Once the Prophet (Peace be upon him) was asked, 'What is the hallmark of the dwellers of Paradise?' The Prophet (Peace be upon him) replied, 'Truthfulness'."

Conversely, a hadiith (tradition) reads:

"'To be a liar is one of the special signs of a hypocrite.' It was asked of the Prophet (Peace be upon him) whether a Believer could be a coward. He said, 'It is possible.' It was asked whether a Believer could be a miser. He said, 'It is possible.' Again, it was asked of him whether a Believer could be a liar. He said, 'No.' (The idea of the Prophet (Peace be upon him) was that a Believer in Allah could not develop the filthy habit of lying. Faith could never accommodate falsehood; they could not go together)."

Fulfilling promises

It is also a part of truthfulness that when a promise is made it should be fulfilled. The Qur-aan and the ahaadiith (traditions) are very clear on the point. Our Faith demands of us never to go back on our pledged word. States the Qur-aan:

"And fulfil (every) engagement, for (every) engagement will be enquired into (on the Day of Reckoning)." — *Surah Israa [Banii Israa-eel] (XVII), 34.*

"To fulfil the contracts which ye have made." — *Surah Baqarah (II), 177.*

56

And the ahaadiith (traditions) say:

"He who does not fulfil promises made by him has no share in Faith."

"Not to fulfil one's promises is a special sign of a hypocrite."

Trustworthiness

Closely allied to truthfulness is the quality of trustworthiness. It is an important branch of it. Islaam has laid special emphasis on it also. Here is what the Qur-aan says:

"Allah doth command you to render back your Trusts to those to whom they are due." — Surah Nisaa (IV), 58.

The Prophet (Peace be upon him) used to say in his sermons :

"People! In whom there is no trustworthiness, in him there is, so to speak, no Faith."

"Look not alone at anyone's prayers and fasts to decide about his spiritual excellence (that is, do not be impressed by anyone's spirituality simply because you find him devout in his prayers and fasts). You should also see that he is truthful when he speaks, restores honestly what he has received in trust to whom it is due, and remains righteous in times of adversity and suffering."

Justice

Justice is an integral part of Islaamic ethics. We must practise it in all spheres of life. The Qur-aan states:

"Allah commands justice and doing of good." — Surah Nahl (XVI), 90.

In Islam we are commanded to be just and fair not only towards our own people or co-religionists but also towards others, even if they be the enemies of our life, property or Faith. It is candidly stated in the Qur-aan that:

"And let not the hatred of others to you make you swerve to wrong and depart from justice. Be just; that is next to piety." — *Surah Maa-i-dah (V), 8.*

The above verse enjoins justice to those also, individuals as well as communities, who may be harbouring ill-will against us. Otherwise, we are sure to incur the displeasure of Allah and become grievous sinners and criminals in His sight.

To refer now to some of the ahaadiith (traditions):

"The most beloved of men in the sight of Allah, on the Day of Resurrection, and the nearest to Him, shall be the just leader; and the most hateful of men in the sight of Allah, on the Day of Resurrection, and the farthest removed from Him, shall be the tyrannical ruler."

"The Prophet (Peace be upon him) is reported to have enquired one day from the Companions: 'Do you know who will be the first to come under the shadow of Divine Mercy on the Day of Requital?' The companions replied, 'Allah and His Apostle know best.' The Prophet (Peace be upon him) then said, 'They will be those who accept a trust when it is offered to them and restore it willingly to the rightful claimant when they are asked to do so, and who judge in respect of others exactly as they would in respect of themselves'."

The pity is that we ourselves have forgotten the glorious teachings of Islaam. If we can produce these qualities within us today, and become truthful in word and deed, and honest in the matter of our trusts and promises, and just and fair in our dealings with others, the success of the world is bound to kiss our feet and we will attain a high place in Paradise too.

Compassion and forgiveness

To feel pity on a fellow human being in distress, to be compassionately drawn towards him, to bring him succour, and to pardon the guilty and the defaulter are virtues that are valued very highly in Islaam. Take these ahaadiith (traditions), for instance:

"Show kindness, and kindness shall be shown to you; forgive, and you shall be forgiven."

"They will not obtain the mercy of Allah in whose hearts there is no feeling of kindness for others."

"His sins will not be forgiven by Allah who does not forgive the faults of others."

"Allah will have mercy upon them that are merciful. Treat kindly the dwellers of the earth, He who dwells in the heavens will treat you kindly."

It is apparent from the last hadiith (tradition) that our kindness and gentility is not to be confined to our own people alone. We ought to be kind and compassionate towards friend and foe alike and to all the creatures that exist on the earth.

It is reported from the Prophet (Peace be upon him) that once a person who was travelling by road saw a dog licking wet earth in the agony of thirst. The traveller was moved by the spectacle and gave water to the dog to drink. This simple service of the man to the thirsting dog pleased Allah so much that He blessed him with salvation.

Tenderness

Tenderness in monetary dealings, and in all other fields of one's activity, and the readiness to oblige and put others at ease, are all virtues of the highest order in the Islaamic pattern of morality. We will reproduce two ahaadiith (traditions) of the noble Prophet (Peace be upon him) in support of our contention. Said he:

"Hell's fire is forbidden for those that are mild and gentle and make it easy for others to deal with them."

"Allah is compassionate and likes compassion in His creatures. He grants more to the kind and the tender-hearted than to those that are harsh and severe."

Self-restraint

Tolerance, affability, self-restraint, and the ability to control one's temper and overlook what is unpleasant and disagreeable, are qualities that Islaam wants everyone to cultivate. Believers who possess these fine moral attributes hold a very high place in the estimation of Allah.

In the Qur-aan where a mention is made of the blessed ones for whom Paradise has been laid out, such people are specifically referred to:

"Who restrain anger and pardon (all men)." — Surah Aali 'Imraan (III), 134.

Said the Prophet (Peace be upon him):

"Allah will hold back His punishment from him who will hold back his anger."

Blessed, indeed, are men who remember these verses and ahaadiith (traditions) during moments of provocation and exercise restraint, and, in return, Allah stays His chastisement from them!

Gentleness of speech

Gentleness of speech is a religious virtue in Islaam and rudeness a sin. The Qur-aan declares:

"Speak fair to the people." — *Surah Baqarah (II), 83.*

We have it from the Prophet (Peace be upon him) that:

"To speak politely is piety and a kind of charity."

"To indulge in intemperate language and in harsh behaviour is to perpetrate an injustice and the home of injustice is Hell."

"Rudeness in speech is hypocrisy (i.e, the quality of a hypocrite)."

Humility

Humility is a virtue. Islaam wants its followers to practise it as a distinguishing feature of their moral and spiritual behaviour. It does not behave a Muslim to be haughty and vainglorious.

Greatness with Allah is not for those who look down upon others. Instead, it belongs to those who desist from thinking too highly of themselves and practise humility. In the words of the Qur-aan:

"And the servants of (Allah) Most gracious are those who walk on the earth in humility." — *Surah Furqaan (XXV), 63.*

"The Home of the hereafter We shall give to those who intend not high-handedness or mischief on earth." — *Surah Qasas (XXVIII), 83.*

The noble Prophet (Peace be upon him) has said:

"He who observes humility Allah will make him so exalted that, ultimately, he will attain the highest grade in Paradise."

On the other hand, pride is so greatly repugnant to Allah that the sacred Prophet (Peace be upon him) has warned us, again and again, against it in such strong words:

61

"Whoever has pride in his heart even of the weight of a mustard seed[1], shall not enter Paradise."

"Beware of pride! Pride was the sin which first of all ruined the devil."

May Almighty Allah save us all from the satanic evil of pride and endow our hearts and minds with meekness and humility which He admires so much and is the symbol of His slaves.

It needs, however, to be remembered that it is demanded of us to practise meekness and humility in our personal matters and not in matters where truth or Faith is involved. When it comes to Faith or truth we must be bold and outspoken and give the fullest proof of courage and firmness, for this is the Will of Allah for such occasions.

The way of a Muslim, in sum, is that while he is meek and humble in his own individual sphere of existence, he is firm like a rock and allows neither fear nor weakness to come near him where Faith or truth or justice is at stake.

Courage and fortitude

There occur periods of hardship and adversity in the lives of men. Sometimes there is want, sometimes there is disease, sometimes our enemies harass us, and, so forth. For such situations the teaching of Islaam is that we should bear them with courage and fortitude, remain firm and stout of heart and do not waver from our principles, in spite of a thousand trials and calamities that may assail us. For such men there is the assurance of the Qur-aan that they are the Beloved of Allah:

"For Allah loves those who are patient and persevering." — *Surah Aaali 'Imraan (III), 146.*

---

1. The word occurring in the original is raa-ee (sinapis remosa) which is a kind of mustard seed with very small grains. — Translator.

"Allah, surely, is with those who patiently persevere." — *Surah Baqarah (II), 153.*

"And to be firm and patient in pain (or suffering) and adversity and through all periods of panic. Such are the people of truth, the Allah-fearing." — *Surah Baqarah (II), 177.*

And the Prophet (Peace be upon him) says:

"No boon conferred on man is more precious than that of patience."

"Patience is one-half of Faith."

Contrarily, impatience, chicken-heartedness and cowardice are the most lamentable of evils against which the Prophet (Peace be upon him) used to beg Allah for refuge in his prayers.

Sincerity

Sincerity is the life and soul of the entire moral edifice of Islaam, nay, of Islaam itself. By sincerity we mean that all our deeds and actions should solely be for the sake of Allah and prompted by no other urge than to earn His countenance. Apart from it, there must be no other desire, motive or intention behind whatever we do.

Monotheism, which is the arch-stone of Islaam attains fulfilment through sincerity. Faith in Divine Unity remains imperfect unless all our acts are performed wholly for the sake of Allah, and we have no other objective before us while carrying them out, except the winning of divine pleasure and reward. States the Prophet (Peace be upon him):

"He who loves or hates, offers favours or withholds them, and whatever he does, does so for the sake of Allah, he perfects his Faith."

It shows that a perfect Muslim in the sight of Allah is only he who succeeds in subordinating his entire conduct, his social relations and all his other, affairs to the Will of Allah and is not influenced in them

63

by personal desire or likes or dislikes or by any other urges or impulsions.

Another hadiith (tradition) reads:

"Allah is not regardful of your fine visages or your wealth. He is regardful only of your hearts and intentions."

The idea of the above hadiith (tradition) is that Allah will judge and requite solely on the basis of our motives and intentions.

Now, here is a hadiith (tradition) with which we propose to round off the present discussion. About this hadiith, it is reported that Sayyidina Abu Hurairah often used to faint while he related it. It says:

"The first of those who shall be called to account, on the Day of Resurrection, shall be one who had learned the Qur-aan by heart, and one who had been killed in the way of Allah, and one who had an abundance of wealth. Then shall Allah say to him who had got the whole of the Qur-aan by heart, 'Did I not teach thee what I revealed to My Prophet?' He will say, 'Yes, my Lord!' Allah will ask, 'And what hast thou done with regard to what thou didst learn therein?' He will say, 'I was constantly at it in the hours of night and in the hours of day. I learnt it myself and taught it, also, to others, and I did it all for Thy sake alone. Allah will say, 'Thou art a liar; thou didst only desire that men should say that such a one was a reciter of the Qur-aan and that has been said already'."

"And the master of wealth shall be brought before Allah, and Allah shall say, 'Did I not give thee an abundance of wealth so that thou wast not in want of anything?' He will say, 'Yes, my Lord!' Allah will say, 'And what hast thou done with what I gave thee?' He will answer, 'I regarded the rights of kinship, and gave alms, and I did so for Thy sake.' Allah will say, 'Thou art a liar; thou didst desire that men should say that such a one was a generous man, and that has been said already'."

64

"Then shall he who had been killed in the way of Allah be brought before Him, and Allah will say to Him, 'What was it that thou wast killed for?' He will reply, 'Thou didst bid us to do jihaad in Thy way, and I fought, and was killed', Allah will say, 'Thou art a liar; thou didst desire that men should say that such a one was a valiant man, and that has been said already'."

"These are the three men who, of all creatures, shall be first sent into Fire."

Brothers, — now, let us examine our thoughts and deeds in the light of the above ḥadiith (tradition) and see where do we stand in the sight of Allah!

O Allah! Endue our hearts with sincerity, and set right our motives and intentions, and make us Thy devoted, dedicated slaves. Aa-miin.

Lesson 10

Love of Allah, the Prophet (Peace be upon him) and the Faith

ISLAAM REQUIRES OF US to believe in Allah and His Apostle, and observe salaah, saum, zakaah and hajj, and lead a life of piety and honesty, and goodness and gentility, and moral and social rectitude and self-discipline. In the same way, it is also one of its fundamental teachings that we should hold Allah, the Prophet (Peace be upon him) and the holy Faith dearer to our hearts than anything else, may it be our parents, children, life, honour or property. In plain words, what it means is that should a time come when it may involve the risk of life, honour or property or of any other worldly thing or interest, to abide by the Faith of Islaam and remain loyal to the injunctions of Allah and the Prophet (Peace be upon him), then we must not break away from Allah and the Prophet (Peace be upon him) and the holy Faith, irrespective of what the consequences may be.

It has been stressed repeatedly in the Qur-aan and the ahaadiith (traditions), that those who may claim to be Muslims but do not possess as strong a devotion for Allah, the Prophet (Peace be upon him) and the Faith as this, are, in fact, not true Muslims. What is more, they are deserving of Divine Chastisement. Reads Surah Taubah:

"Say: 'If it be that your fathers, your sons, your brothers, your mates, or your kindred: the wealth that ye have gained; the commerce in which ye fear a decline; or the dwellings in which ye delight are dearer to you than Allah, and His Apostle, or the striving in His cause; then wait until Allah brings about His decision: and Allah guides not the rebellious'."
— Surah Taubah (IX), 24.

Those who love their parents or children or life or honour or property, more than they love Allah, and care more for their

66

protection and well-being than for His good pleasure, and for the defence and progress of His Faith, are unquestionably disloyal to Allah and worthy of His punishment. A ḥadiiṯẖ (tradition) says:

"He alone will taste the sweetness of Faith who possesses these three qualities: the love of Allah and the Prophet (Peace be upon him) comes to him before everything else; he loves whom he loves solely for the sake of Allah; and the idea of going back to apostasy after he has embraced Islaam is as repugnant to him as being thrown into the fire."

In the sight of Allah and the Prophet (Peace be upon him), a true and commited Muslim is a person whose devotion to Allah and His Apostle and Faith is stronger than to any other person or thing in the world, so much so, that when he loves any other human being he loves him for the sake of Allah, and who is so sincerely and powerfully attached to the Islaamic faith that the very thought of leaving it and reverting back to apostasy may be as painful to him as being cast into the fire.

"Says the Prophet (Peace be upon him): 'None of you can be an honest Muslim and a truthful believer unless his love for me exceeds the love he has for his parents, children or any other human being in the world'."

Brothers, — Islaam really is nothing besides surrender and submission to Allah and the Prophet (Peace be upon him) with all one's heart and soul, and the readiness to sacrifice every attachment, longing or interest for the sake of Faith, as the noble Companions had done, and as the state is of the true and devoted bondsmen of the Lord even today, however small their number may be. May we, also, be one of them!

Lesson 11

Preaching and propagation

ESSENTIAL AS IT IS for us to affirm faith in Allah and the Prophet (Peace be upon him) and to follow with righteousness and sincerity the straight path of Islaam, it is also of no mean importance that we strive earnestly to guide others, too, to the path of Faith who are ignorant of it or who may be unwilling to adopt it on account of prejudice or spiritual malaise. As Allah has placed on us the duty of being His pious, devout and faithful servants, so also has He made it obligatory for us to work among His other creatures as well towards the same end, that is, towards making them also His pious, devout and faithful bondsmen. That is what is meant by the service of Faith and its preaching and propagation.

This work is so great in the sight of Allah that for it He sent down thousands of Prophets into the world. The Prophets bore tremendous hardships and went through the severest of trials and privations to carry out their mission. They worked for the moral and spiritual reform and upliftment of mankind. (May the eternal blessings of Allah be on them and their companions and supporters).

The glorious chain of Prophecy and Apostleship ended with the last of the Prophets, the Prophet Muḥammad (Peace and Blessings of Allah be upon him). Through him also Allah proclaimed to the world that no more Prophets would now be raised up for the guidance of humanity. The celestial mission shall now be carried on by those who have accepted his guidance and the religion he had brought with him into the world.

In sum, after the termination of the luminous line of apostles, the responsibility for preaching and propagation of Faith and religious instruction and reform of mankind has fallen wholly upon the shoulders of the followers of the sacred Prophet (Peace be upon him).

This honour, indeed, is unique. In the Qur-aan, the very object of the raising up of Muslims has been defined as nothing but this:

"You are the best of Peoples, evolved for mankind, enjoining what is right, forbidding what is wrong and believing in Allah." — Surah Aali 'Imraan III), 110.

The Muslims are, thus, superior to all other peoples and communities for the simple reason that they, in addition to adopting for themselves the path of Faith and righteousness, are charged with the special duty of striving to bring others also to practise what is right and to avoid what is wrong. It is because of this that they are given the distinction of being the 'Best of Peoples'. It is, also, evident from the above verse that, should the Muslims fail to discharge the function, they would not only forfeit the claim but also render themselves liable to be punished by Allah for neglecting the duty He had assigned to them. Let us take an illustration: Suppose a company of sentries is posted in a town by the government to check the immoral activities of its citizens, and the sentries not only fail to perform their duty but, what is more, they themselves begin to indulge in the transgressions they were required to suppress. Now, will they be retained in service and rewarded by the government, or taken severely to task by it for their negligence and misconduct? It will, certainly, not be improper or unjust if they were punished more severely than the other offenders.

The conditions prevailing in the entire Muslim World today are so extremely deplorable that, to speak of the preaching of Faith and correction and reform of others, not more than five or ten per cent of Muslims themselves are true to Islaam and do good deeds and abstain from what is evil and prohibited. In these circumstances, it becomes our primary duty to carry out the mission of moral and spiritual reform and guidance among our own people — among such sections of them as have drifted regretfully away from the path of Faith and moral uprightness.

69

One of the reasons for it is that those who call themselves, or are known as Muslims, whatever be their practical state, have, after all, forged a link between themselves and Allah and His Prophet (Peace be upon him) and Faith, and become members of the Muslim brotherhood or ummah, through the acceptance of Islaam. Solicitude for their moral and spiritual well-being is our first responsibility, in any case, in the same way as the responsibility of looking after the welfare of his own children and near relations is greater on a man than that of looking after the welfare of others.

And, secondly, before everything else, it is the actual condition of Muslims from which the world will generally judge about Islaam, and the spectacle of degeneration that Muslims, on the whole, present these days is such that it cannot be expected to make a very favourable impression on anyone in respect of their Faith. The non-Muslim World is not likely to think very highly of the excellent teachings of Islaam as long as Muslims remain what they are today. On the other hand, it is a feeling of revulsion and dislike which non-Muslims usually get about Islaam when they look at the moral and spiritual depths into which the Muslims have sunk. It has always been like this. People have always formed their opinion, good or bad or indifferent, about a religion, from the actual moral and social state of its followers.

In the past when Muslims used to be truthful Muslims, observing strictly the postulates of their Faith, people were attracted towards Islaam simply by seeing them. Whole nations and communities were converted to Islaam in this way. But since the Muslims sank so low that the majority of them remained Muslims only in name, their conduct and morals grew un-Islaamic and their hearts went bereft of Faith and righteousness, the world has developed a prejudice against Islaam itself.

Anyhow, we should realise the truth of it clearly that the daily life of Muslims, their social and moral and spiritual conduct and behaviour, is the biggest testimony and the chief measuring rod with regard to Islaam. If the practical life of Muslims is good, the world will form a good opinion about Islaam and, if it is bad, the latter case, the preaching of Islaam among non-Muslims is destined to be fruitless. Hence, the success of all the efforts aimed at the propagation of Islaam among non-Muslims as well, is dependent on the condition that Islaamic life, i.e., the life of Faith and righteous action become the chief attribute of the entire Muslim community. From this point of view, also, it is necessary to strive first for the guidance and reformation of Muslims, and to launch the struggle with all our might for popularising the values of Islaamic life among them, before we turned our attention to others.

The Qur-aan has given the task of religious preaching, reform and guidance the name of jihaad akbar, the great jihaad[1]. If it is undertaken in the right spirit, with sincerity and selflessness, and solely for the sake of winning divine approbation, this work, definitely is a very great jihaad in the sight of Allah.

Many people suppose that jihaad means only a war which is waged in the path of Allah and according to the rules and instructions laid down for it in the sharii'ah. But it is not correct. The truth is that whatever endeavour that can be made at a particular time for the preaching and propagation of Islaam and moral and spiritual correction and guidance of mankind, is jihaad of that age.

The noble Prophet (Peace be upon him) remained in Makkah for about twelve years after the mantle of Apostleship had fallen upon him. During this period, jihaad of the Prophet (Peace be upon him) and his Companions consisted altogether in adhering steadfastly to Faith in spite of the terrible persecution unleashed on them by the enemies of Islaam, and in doing all that lay in their power, openly as

---

1. The commentators of the Qur-aan are generally agreed that the verse, 'Strive against them with the utmost strenuousness (with the Qur-aan)' of Surah Furqaan means the preaching and propagation of Islaam.

71

well as secretly, to spread the Divine Message of Islaam and reform, morally and spiritually, those who lived around them.

To devote oneself to the noble task of guiding the ignorant, the wayward and the thoughtless, to the straight path of Islaam, and of bringing them nearer to Allah, to spend one's time and money on it, to sacrifice one's comfort, all this, in any case, is jihaad in divine estimation. In fact, it is the jihaad of the present age.

The rich reward that awaits those in the hereafter who engage themselves in the lofty endeavour, as well as the dreadful punishment that is going to fall to the lot of those who neglect it and do not participate in it, can well be imagined from the ahaadiith (traditions) we give below:

"A person who guides another to a deed of virtue shall receive the same recompense for it as the doer of the deed, and there will be no reduction in the reward of the doer himself because of it."

What the hadiith (tradition) means is that suppose ten persons, or even five, were reformed through our efforts and they came to believe in Allah and the Prophet (Peace be upon him) and to observe the Divine Commandments, they began to offer salaah and carry out other religious duties and avoided what was wrong and forbidden — then the reward they will earn on it jointly will be granted to us also. A little thought will show that there is simply no other way in which a person can win so much reward — the reward of the prayers and other pious and virtuous deeds of hundreds of men.

Another hadiith (tradition) of the noble Prophet (Peace be upon him) says:

"By the Almighty, if only one man receives guidance through you, it is better for you than red camels."[1]

----

1. The Arabs in those days placed a very high value on red camels.

As we have said earlier, the endeavour for mankind's moral and spiritual guidance and reformation is a service of Faith of the highest order and a thing of outstanding merit and excellence. It is the special heritage left to us by the Prophets. It means their deputyship; it means their vicegerency. What worldly gain, what earthly glory, can compare with it?

The noble Prophet (Peace be upon him), in the undermentioned hadiith, has made use of a simple example to impress upon us the importance of the work of religious reformation and guidance.

"He said, 'Suppose there is a double storeyed boat in which passengers of the lower deck have to fetch water from the upper deck. This causes inconvenience to the occupants of the upper deck and they do not like it. Now, if in their foolishness the passengers of the lower deck decide not to go to the upper deck for their supply of water, and begin to bore a hole in the bottom of the boat, and the passengers of the upper deck do not stop them from doing so, the entire boat, with all the passengers, will sink. But if the occupants of the upper deck, somehow, manage to dissuade the occupants of the lower deck from boring the hole, they will save the occupants of the lower deck, as well as themselves from being drowned. The same is true with wickedness and sin. If a community, as a whole, dwells in a state of ignorance and sinfulness, and its enlightened and virtuous sections do not take steps to reform it and to bring it on the right path, then Divine Punishment will be sent down upon it because of its sins and transgressions, and the pious and virtuous members of the community will, also, be caught in it. On the other hand, if an endeavour is made by them to reform the sinners and wrongdoers, the whole community will be saved.' "

Again, the Prophet (Peace be upon him) is reported to have said:

"By the Almighty in whose power lies my life, do not neglect the duty of enjoining what is right and forbidding what is wrong. Remember if you neglected your duty, it is quite possible that Allah

73

sent down His punishment on you, and then all your prayers and supplications will be in vain."

Brothers, — some of the most enlightened and spiritually evolved divines of our day are of the view that the disasters and humiliations that have been visiting Muslims for a long time, and the troubles and difficulties they are caught in universally these days, and which do not seem to abate or relent a bit, in spite of their pathetic petitions to Allah and prayers etc., are due mainly to the very reason that they have ceased to discharge the function they were raised up for and for which they were made wholly responsible after the termination of Prophecy and Apostleship. Evidently, when a watchman fails to perform his duty, he is dismissed from service and castigated sternly for his negligence.

Come, let us resolve solemnly that we shall be found wanting no more in the discharge of our duty. Allah's help will be with us. He has promised:

"Allah, certainly, will aid those who aid His Cause." — *Surah Hajj (XXII), 40.*

Lesson 12

Constancy

ONE OF THE SPECIAL responsibilites a man owes to Allah, once he has accepted the faith of Islaam, is that he remains firm and steadfast in Faith at all times and in all circumstances. He is expected to uphold the Faith with all his courage and strength, however adverse the conditions may be. He should not prove disloyal to Islaam in any event. He must not give it up. This is what is meant by 'Constancy of Faith'. Such men have been spoken of very highly in the Qur-aan and a bountiful reward has been promised to them in the hereafter. It says:

"In the case of those who say, 'Our Lord is Allah, and, further, stand straight and steadfast, the angels descend on them (from time to time): Fear ye not (they suggest), nor grieve! But receive the tidings of the Garden (of Bliss), which ye were promised! We are your protectors in this life and in the hereafter! Therein shall ye have all that your souls will desire! Therein shall ye have all that ye ask for! A hospitable gift from One, Oft-Forgiving, Most Merciful!'" — Surah Fussilat (XLI), 30-31.

What wonderful tidings does the above verses contain for those who are constant in Faith and patiently persevere and remain steadfast in times of misfortune and peril. If one could attain this position, even at the cost of one's life, property and everything, it would not be a bad bargain indeed.

It is related that once a Companion asked the Prophet (Peace be upon him) to tell him something that could suffice for him always and after which he would not have the need to turn for advice to anyone. The Prophet (Peace be upon him) said, "Say, 'Allah (alone) is my Lord', and stick to it (i.e., conduct your life in accordance with it unswervingly)."

75

For our benefit and guidance, a number of extremely inspiring parables have been narrated in the Qur-aan of devout and faithful servants of Allah who remained true to faith in circumstances of utmost distress and suffering. Neither fear nor greed could make them deviate from the path they had chosen. One such parable is of the magicians of Egypt who were summoned to challenge Prophet Musaa (Moses) (Peace be upon him) and great rewards and honours had been promised to them. Yet, after the truth of Divine Inspiration and the apostolic message of Musaa (Moses) (Peace be upon him) had dawned upon them, they cared neither for the riches and honours the Fir'aun (Pharaoh) had promised, nor for the savage punishment they were sure to receive at his hands for disobeying his commands. Rising above the considerations of gain or loss, they boldly declared before the vast assembly of men, "We believe in the Lord of Haaruun (Aaron) and Musaa (Moses)." Later, when they were threatened by that enemy of Allah, the Pharaoh, that he would have their arms and legs severed, and then they would be hanged on the gallows, they replied dauntlessly, displaying magnificent courage of conviction that:

"So decree whatever thou desirest to decree: for thou canst decree (touching) only the life of this world. For us, we have believed in our Lord: May He forgive us our sins." — Surah Ṯaa Haa (XX), 72-73.

Still more inspiring is the story of Pharaoh's wife. You know that Pharaoh was the all-powerful monarch of Egypt whose wife was the sole mistress of his heart. From this you can imagine how enviable would have been her lot. All the world's glories and luxuries were at her feet. Yet when the innermost depths of her soul were stirred by the divine call of Musaa (Moses) (Peace be upon him), she did not give a thought to what her husband would do to her or how her life of cloudless bliss would change into that of colossal distress and misery. Regardless of the consequences, she proclaimed her faith and once she had done so, she flinched not from the path of duty towards Allah and religion, though the torture she was subjected to was simply barbarous, the very idea of which is enough to make our flesh

76

creep even today. In return for it, such a unique honour was conferred on her by Allah that her name has been mentioned reverentially in the Qur-aan and the patient perseverance displayed by her and her sacrifice have been held forth as an example to all Muslims.

"And Allah sets forth, as an example to those who believe, the wife of Pharaoh: behold, she said! 'Build for me in nearness to Thee, a mansion in the Garden, and save me from Pharaoh and his doings, and save me from those that do wrong." — Surah Tah̲riim (LXVI), 11.

Glory be! What rare honour, what matchless distinction, really, that Allah has chosen the constancy of faith of that blessed lady to serve as an example to the entire ummah, from Sayyidina Abu Bakr down to the last generation of Muslims before the Last Day.

It is related that when the atrocities perpetrated by the polytheists of Makkah on Muslims exceeded all limits and the Companions approached the august Prophet (Peace be upon him) to pray to Allah for mercy and protection, the Prophet (Peace be upon him) remarked, "You have become disheartened so soon! Men of Allah before you were subjected to such brutal torture that combs of red hot iron were driven into their heads, and the skulls of some of them were sawed off into two and yet they remained steadfast and did not abandon their Faith."

Lesson 13

Jihaad

THE BELIEVERS ARE REQUIRED emphatically to do whatever they can towards popularising, defending and keeping alive and flourishing, as the best and the truest way of life, the way of Islaam and servility to Allah they have chosen for themselves. This, in Islaam, is called jihaad. It can take many forms, depending on the circumstances varying from time to time and place to place.

Suppose there arises a situation in which it becomes difficult or even dangerous for a person or his family or community to profess Islaam and remain true to it, or to be a Muslim may become the hardest thing to do in the world, in that case jihaad will lie in doing one's best for oneself, one's family or community to stay firmly devoted to Islaam. It would, certainly, be a most splendid jihaad in those circumstances. Similarly, should Muslims, through their own folly or negligence, start drifting away from Faith, then, at such a time, to devote one's time and energy to their religious revival and reform, too, would constitute a kind of jihaad.

To carry the Divine Guidance to those that are ignorant of it, and to make an earnest effort to persuade them wisely and sympathetically to accept it, is yet another form of jihaad.

Should believers in Allah and the Prophet (Peace be upon him) be in power somewhere and the conditions demand that collective force be used for the defence and assistance of Faith, then, in that case, the use of force for the defence and assistance of Faith, according to the rules laid down for it, will constitute jihaad. Two conditions, however, are essential for it. Firstly, such a step must not be motivated by any personal or national self-interest, greed or enmity. It should be taken solely to carry out the command of Allah and to serve the cause of His Faith. And, secondly, that the rules prescribed for it were scrupulously observed. If force is used without the fulfilment of these conditions, it will not be jihaad according to Islaam but wanton wickedness and mischief.

To speak a just word before a tyrannical ruler (be he a Muslim or a non-Muslim) is, again, a form of jihaad. In the ahaadiith (traditions) it has been spoken as "The best of jihaad."

All these forms of religious struggle and endeavour, at their proper time and place, are among the obligatory duties of Islaam, and, as we have seen, the term jihaad is applied to them in various degrees.

We now proceed to examine some of the verses of the Qur-aan and the ahaadiith (traditions) of the Prophet (Peace be upon him) enjoining on Muslims the duty of jihaad and revealing to them what unique glory and spiritual merit lies in it. First, the Qur-aanic verses:

"And strive in His cause as ye ought to strive (with sincerity and under discipline). He has chosen you." — Surah Hajj (XXII), 78.

"O ye who believe! shall I lead you to a bargain that will save you from a grievous penalty? That ye believe in Allah and his Apostle, and that ye strive (your utmost) in the cause of Allah, with your property and your persons: that will be best for ye if ye but knew! He will forgive ye your sins and admit ye to Gardens beneath which rivers flow, and to beautiful mansions in Gardens of Eternity: that is, indeed, the Supreme Achievement." — Surah Saff (LXI), 10-12.

After these, the ahaadiith (traditions):

"To believe truthfully in Allah and to strive in the path of Faith is the best of all deeds."

"I shall not be that a person whose feet are covered with dust in the path of Allah went to Hell."

"For anyone of you to rise in the way of Allah (i.e., in the defence of Islaam and to take some part in the struggle for its progress and glory) is better than seventy years of worship in the corner of his house."

May it be allotted to us also by Allah to earn the divine reward that is for those who make earnest exertions in the path of His Faith!

Lesson 14

Martyrdom

IN THE SPECIAL LANGUAGE of Islaam a person who meets his death in the cause of Faith, either as a result of obeying its injunctions and carrying out its commands as a staunch and devoted follower, or in the course of struggle for its defence, is called a martyr. For such a man there is a place of unparalleled honour and distinction in the hereafter. His lot is truly divine. About the martyrs it is said in the Qur-aan that they should not be thought of as dead: they are alive, a very special existence is conferred on them and they are the recipients of boundless favours and blessings from their Lord.

"Think not of those who are slain in Allah's way as dead. Nay, they live, finding their sustenance in the Presence of their Lord." — Surah Aali 'Imraan (III), 169.

How marvellous is the fate of these true and noble sons of Islaam, how mightily beloved of Allah they are, and what glorious rewards are showered upon them by Him can be visualised from the ḥadiith (tradition) we are now going to reproduce. The noble Prophet (Peace be upon him) is reported to have said:

"No one among the dwellers of Paradise will ever want to be sent back to the world, although all the worldly joys and riches may be his if he is sent back, except one who has been killed in the way of Allah; such a man will want to be returned to the earth and be killed in the cause of Allah ten times over, because of the high honour and splendid ceremony with which he will be received in Heaven on account of dying a martyr's death."

The sacred Prophet (Peace be upon him) himself was so enthusiastic about attaining martyrdom that he often used to say:

"By the Holy Being in whose power lies my life, I wish I was killed in Allah's way and brought back to life and killed once more and brought back to life and this happened to me over and over again." Another of the Prophet's (Peace be upon him) ahaadiith (traditions) reads:

"Six rewards are conferred on a martyr by Allah: one, he is forgiven immediately and his abode in Paradise is shown to him; two, he is spared the punishment of the grave; third, he is granted freedom from the acute fear and anxiety of the Day of Requital that will grip the heart of every one (except those on whom there will be the favour of the Lord); four, a crown of honour will be placed on his head, a single ruby of which will be more valuable than the whole world; five, seventy-two celestial brides will be given to him in marriage; and, six, his intercession will be accepted on behalf of seventy kinsmen."

Furthermore:"To fall a martyr in the cause of Allah atones for everything except a debt."

And, it should be remembered that the divine reward and other wonderful favours promised on martyrdom are not dependent only on death occurring in the way of Allah. It is not that when a person is killed in the cause of Allah, only then does he become entitled to them. Every loss or injury suffered, every pain and suffering undergone, in the service of Faith, carries a bounteous reward. Any Believer who may be persecuted, punished, beaten, insulted or tortured for the sake of Islaam, will be rewarded most lavishly in the hereafter. Allah will raise him so high in honour that the most exalted of saints and divines will envy his fate. Just as soldiers, in this world, who serve their motherland gallantly and care nothing for their own safety when the call of duty comes, are honoured with awards and decorations by their governments. In the same way, the servants of Allah who suffer loss or humiliation for the sake of Faith, occupy a special place of glory in the celestial scheme of things. On the Day of Recompense when these blessed children of Islaam will receive their awards and decorations and the Almighty will honour them with His exquisite favours and bounties, all the rest of men will regretfully wish they, too, had undergone a similar experience in the world, that they, too, had been punished, tortured and humiliated for the sake of Faith so that they would also have got those magnificent favours and rewards on that Day.

Should a trial of this kind be destined for us as well, O Lord, at that fateful hour, keep us brave and steadfast and withhold not from us Thy grace!

Lesson 15

Life after death

THIS MUCH IS KNOWN to everyone, that whoever is born into the world has got to die one day or another. But nobody knows on his own what happens or will happen after death. This is known only to Allah. Allah vouchsafes the knowledge of it to His Prophets (Peace be upon them) and through the Prophets men like you and me also come to know about it. Every Prophet of Allah, in his time, had revealed clearly to his people through what stages they would have to pass after death and how at each stage they would be recompensed for their deeds — good as well as bad — during the earthly sojourn. Since the Prophet Muḥammad (Peace and Blessings of Allah be upon him) is the last of the divine apostles and messengers, and no prophet is going to be raised up after him, the different stages through which a man has to pass after death have been explained by him in greatest detail and with utmost clarity. If all that the Prophet (Peace be upon him) has revealed in this connection is brought together, it would make a volume by itself. We will, therefore, give a very brief summary of it here.

There are to follow three stages after death. The first stage runs from death to Resurrection. It is called barzakh[1]. Whether a person is buried when he dies or he is cremated or cast into the river, his soul does not perish with him. It is immortal; it lives. It only migrates from the material world of ours to another world. In this other world the angels question him about his spiritual state. If he is a truthful believer, he gives the correct answers whereupon the angels impart to him the glad tidings that he is going to live in peace and happiness till the Last Day. And, if it is otherwise, that is, he turns out to be an unbeliever, an infidel or a sham or hypocritical Muslim, he is, at

---

1. The interval between death and resurrection. — Translator.

once, placed under dreadful punishment which is not to cease before the Day of Reckoning.

The next stage comprises of the last day and the resurrection. The last day means that there will come a time when the entire material world will be destroyed by the command of Allah. Annihilation will descend suddenly on everything that exists around us. The whole world will be thrown topsyturvy. Then, after a long time, when Allah will wish, all men will be raised up again. Every person born into the world will be re-created and called upon to render a full account of his doings on earth. In the Great Reckoning, those who will be found worthy of deliverance, will be awarded a place in Paradise, and those who will turn out to be guilty and deserving of Divine Chastisement, will be consigned to Hell.

After this, there will commence the last stage. The dwellers of Paradise will live in a state of eternal bliss, supremely immune from every kind of pain, anxiety and suffering, and exulting in the bounties of their Lord, the like of which they would not have dreamt of in the world, while those that will be condemned to Hell will have to live permanently in a condition of unmitigated misery and distress. There will be for them nothing but horrible agony and fearful castigation. This will be the ultimate stage after death.

The above was the sum and substance of what the Prophets, specially the last of them, the Prophet Muhammad (Peace be upon him), have taught mankind about the hereafter and what is indicated about it in the Qur-aan and the ahaadiith (traditions). We will now examine some of the relevant verses of the Qur-aan:

"Every soul shall have a taste of death: in the end to Us shall ye be brought back." — Surah 'Ankabuut (XXIX), 57.

"Every soul shall have a taste of death: and on the Day of Judgement shall you be paid your full recompense." — Surah Aali 'Imraan (III), 185.

The Last Day will be a frightful, horrible day.

85

"O mankind! fear your Lord! for the convulsion of the Hour (of Judgement) will be a thing terrible! the day ye shall see it: every nursing mother shall forget her suckling babe, and every pregnant female shall drop her load unformed! thou shall see mankind as in a drunken riot, yet not drunk! but dreadful shall be the wrath of Allah." — Surah Hajj (XXII), 1-2.

"One day the earth and the mountains will be in violent commotion and the mountains will be as a heap of sand poured out and flowing down." — Surah Muzzammil (LXXIII), 14.

"A day that will make children hoary-headed." — Surah Muzzammmil (LXXIII), 17.

"At length, when there comes the deafening noise, that day shall a man flee from his own brothers, and from his mother and his father, and from his wife and children. Each of them, that day, will have enough concern (of his own) to make him indifferent to other. Some faces that day will be beaming, laughing, rejoicing. And other faces that day will be dust-stained; blackness will cover them... ." — Surah 'A-bas (LXXX), 33-41.

On the Day of Recompense:

"That day shall ye be brought to Judgement! not an act of yours that ye hide will be hidden." — Surah Haaqqah (LXIX), 18.

"One day We shall remove the mountains, and thou will see the earth as a level stretch, and We shall gather them, altogether, nor shall We leave out any of them. And they will be marshalled before the Lord in ranks, with the announcement, 'Now have ye come to Us (bare) as We created ye first! Aye, ye thought We shall not fulfil the appointment made to you to meet Us?' And the Book (of Deeds) will be placed before you; and thou wilt see the sinful in great terror because of what is recorded therein; they will say 'Ah! Woe to us! What a book is this! It leaves nothing small or great, but takes account thereof!' They will find all that they did placed before them; and not one will thy Lord treat with injustice." — Surah Kahf (XVIII), 47-49.

A man's own limbs will depose against him before Allah on the Day of Reckoning.

*"Today We shall set a seal on their mouths. But their hands will speak to Us,
— and their feet will bear witness to all that they did." — Surah Yaa Siin
(XXXVI) 65.*

The Qur-aan, has portrayed most graphically and vividly, the
happenings of the Last Day: the terrific explosions and the dreadful
tremors, the total annihilation of the world — even the mountains
will be wiped out of existence, the rising again of men, the gathering
together of them for the Judgement, the presentation of the Book of
Deeds, the deposing of one's own limbs against oneself, the
Judgement, and, finally, the execution of the Divine Verdict and
the allotment of Heaven and Hell. All these events have been
described so candidly in some of the chapters of the Qur-aan that one
can obtain a full picture of the happenings of the Last Day by reading
them. The Prophet (Peace be upon him), is reported to have
observed, "Anyone who wishes to know about the Last Day as if
the scene of it was drawn before his eyes should read these chapters
of the Qur-aan: Takwiir, Infitaar and Inshiqaaq."

We will now see a few ahaadiith (traditions) of the Prophet (Peace
be upon him) pertaining to barzakh and the Last Day. Says he:

"When anyone of you dies, the place that is going to be his abode
in Heaven or in Hell (on the basis of his conduct in the world), is
brought before his eyes every morning and evening, and it is said to
him, 'Behold, this is your destination, and, surely, you will reach it'."

"When the Trumpet will first be sounded on the Last Day by the
command of Allah everyone will faint and drop dead on the ground.
When it will be sounded next all men will rise again. They will then
be commanded to proceed to make their presence before the Lord.
The angels, thereafter, will be told to collect them together and here
the investigation into their conduct on earth will begin."

"It is related that a Companion once enquired from the Prophet
(Peace be upon him), 'O Messenger of Allah, how will Allah raise up
his creatures from the dead? Is there anything like it here in this
world which may be cited as an example?' The Prophet (Peace be

87

upon him) replied, 'Has it never occurred to you that you passed by a stretch of land in your country and found it dry and bereft of all vegetation, and then, coming upon it again, after some time, discovered that it was covered lavishly with fresh, green grass?' The Companion replied, 'Yes, my master, it has.' The Prophet (Peace be upon him) remarked, 'This typifies resurrection. Allah will raise from the dead in the same manner'."

"The Prophet (Peace be upon him) is reported to have asked, after reciting the Qur-aanic verse, "*On the day (the earth) will declare her tidings.*" — *Surah Zilzaal (XCIX), 4.* 'Do you know what it means?' The Companions are said to have replied, 'Allah and His apostle knows best.' The Prophet (Peace be upon him), the hadii<u>th</u> (tradition) goes on to tell, then, said, 'On the Day of Judgement the earth will bear witness to all the deeds performed by men on it (i.e., at the bidding of Allah the earth will tell that such-and-such a person had done such-and-such a thing on it on such-and-such a day)'."

"Speaking of the Day of Recompense, the Prophet (Peace be upon him), further, is reported to have said, 'On that day Allah will call upon everyone to come forward and be his own witness.' He will say to him, 'To-day you are your own witness: Our recording angels are present; this much of evidence is enough'. Then by the command of Allah the lips of the person will become sealed and he will not be able to utter a word. His limbs (arms, legs etc.,) will then be commanded to speak and they will relate the whole story of his doings in the world."

"It is reported that once a person went to the Prophet (Peace be upon him) and said, 'O Messenger of Allah, I have some slaves who, sometimes, disobey me, or they steal or tell me a lie. I sometimes scold them, and sometimes, I also punish them. How is it going to turn out for me on the Day of Requital?' The Prophet (Peace be upon him) observed, 'Allah will dispense justice correctly on the Day of Judgement. If the punishment you mete out to them is proportionate to their faults you will neither get nor have to give anything; you will be quits. If the punishment turns out to be of a lesser degree than what they merited, you will be recompensed for it. If the punishment proves to be excessive, you will have to recompense the slaves.' On hearing the Prophet's (Peace be upon him) reply the enquirer began to cry. He said, 'Then, O Prophet of Allah, the best thing for me is to send them away. I declare before you that I have set them free.' The Prophet (Peace be upon him) is also reported to have recited the following verse of the Qur-aan to him:

"We shall set up scales of justice for the Day of Judgement, so that not a soul will be dealt with unjustly in the least. And if there be (no more than) the weight of a mustard seed, We will bring it (to account)! and enough are We to take account." — Surah Ambiyaa (XXI), 47.

Lesson 16

Heaven and Hell

IN THE PRECEDING CHAPTER it has been said that the Last Day will be the Day of Judgement. On that day, the believers who will also have done good deeds in the world and on whom there will be no punishment, will rejoice. During the entire proceedings of the day they will rest secure under the shade of divine benevolence and gain immediate admission into Paradise. Such of them as will be adjudged worthy of deliverance but only after they have undergone a spell of punishment, will be forgiven and admitted into Paradise after they have suffered some of the agonies of the Day of Reckoning, or, at the utmost, after they have spent some time in Hell. In any case, those possessing the least amount of faith will, sooner or later, find their place in Heaven. Only men who will have departed from the world in a state of infidelity or polytheism will be doomed to live permanently in Hell. In sum, Heaven is the reward for Faith, fidelity and good-doing, and Hell for infidelity, polytheism and revolt against Allah and transgression against His Will.

The superlative, incomparable blissfulness of Heaven and the fearful, loathsome punishment and torture of Hell have been described in proper detail in the Qur-aan:

"For righteous are Gardens in nearness to their Lord, with rivers flowing beneath; therein is their eternal home; with Companions pure (and holy); and the good pleasure of Allah. For in Allah's sight are (all) His servants."
— Surah Aali 'Imraan (III), 15.

"Verily the Companions of Garden shall that day have joy in all that they do; they and their associates will be in grove of (cool shade; reclining on Thrones (of dignity); every fruit (enjoyment) will be there for them; they shall have whatever they call for; "Peace!" - a word (of salutation) from a Lord Most Merciful." — Surah Yaa Siin (XXXVI), 55-57.

"There will be in there all the souls could desire, all that the eyes could delight in; and ye shall abide therein (forever)." — Surah Zu<u>kh</u>-ruf *(XLIII), 71.*

"(Here is) a parable of the Garden which the righteous are promised. In it are rivers of water incorruptible; rivers of milk of which the taste never changes; rivers of wine of joy to those who drink; and rivers of honey (pure and clear). In it there are for them all kinds of fruits; and Grace from their Lord." — Surah Mu<u>h</u>ammad *(XLVII), 15.*

"No sense of fatigue shall touch them." — Surah <u>H</u>ijr *(XV), 48.*

In short, Heaven is the abode of supreme and eternal blissfulness, felicity and happiness. There will not be the faintest trace of pain, sorrow or distress in it. Let us now see how life in Hell will be like:

"But those whose balance is light, will be those who have lost their souls; in Hell they will abide. The fire will burn their faces, and they will therein grin with their lips displaced." — Surah Mu-minuun *(XXIII), 103-4.*

"For the wrong-doers We have prepared a Fire whose (smoke and flames), like the walls and roof of a tent will hem them in: if they implore relief they will be granted water like melted brass, that will scald their faces." — Surah Kahf *(XVIII), 29.*

"But those who deny (their Lord), for them will be cut out a garment of Fire; over their heads will be poured out boiling water. With it will be scalded what is within their bodies, as well as (their skins). In addition, there will be maces of iron (to punish) them. Every time they wish to get away therefrom, from anguish, they will be forced back therein, and (it will be said). 'Taste ye the Penalty of Burning!' " — Surah <u>H</u>ajj *(XXII), 19-22.*

"Verily the tree of zaqqum will be the food of the sinful, like molten brass; it will boil in their insides, like the boiling of scalding water. (A voice will cry:) 'Seize him and drag him into the midst of the Blazing Fire! Then pour over his head the penalty of Boiling Water." — Surah Du<u>kh</u>-<u>kh</u>aan *(XLIV), 43-48.*

"And he is given for drink boiling fetid water. In gulps will he sip it, but never will be near swallowing it down his throat. Death will come to him

from every quarter, yet will he not die; and in front of him will be a chastisement unrelenting." — *Surah Ibraahiim (XIV), 16-17.*

"Those who reject Our Signs, We shall soon cast into the Fire, as often as their skins are roasted through. We shall change them for fresh skins that they may taste the penalty." — *Surah Nisaa (IV), 56.*

But enough. There are hundreds of verses in the Qur-aan that tell the same story. To take now some of the ahaadii̱th (traditions) of the Prophet (Peace be upon him): "Says Allah, 'For My faithful servants I have got ready (in Heaven) things no eye has seen, nor ear heard of, nor the thought of which has ever crossed a human heart'."

The delicious foods, the luscious fruit, the delightful drinks, the gorgeous clothes, the magnificent palaces, the splendid gardens, the delectable lakes, the wonderful ẖouris (celestial brides) and other innumerable things of divine beauty and joy that will be available in Heaven are, to be sure, known only to Allah. We, on our part, believe in them implicitly and hold them to be absolutely true.

Says another ẖadii̱th (tradition): "As the dwellers will enter Heaven, a heavenly herald will proclaim 'Stay healthy; disease is not going to touch you here. Live forever; death for you exists no more. Remain young; you shall not grow old in Heaven. Be happy always; for you, now, there is neither pain nor sorrow'."

"When the dwellers of Paradise have entered the home of celestial bliss, Allah will enquire from them thus: 'Do you want that I may bestow a favour upon you over and above the blessings you enjoy?' The people of Heaven will answer: 'Our Lord! Thou hast illumined our faces, saved us from Hell and granted us Paradise. [What more can we want?]' The veil will, then, be lifted and they shall see their Lord unhindered. All the endless joys and blessings of Paradise will fade away before the glorious spectacle of the Almighty."

In another ẖadii̱th (tradition) it is related that once the Prophet (Peace be upon him) while describing the marvellous pleasures of the Paradise and the extreme agony of Hell observed:

92

"On the Day of Judgement a person will be brought who will have lived in greatest pomp and luxury in the world, but will be condemned to Hell because of his evil deeds. He will be dipped once into the fire of Hell and then taken out of it immediately and asked, 'Have you ever known comfort?' The man will reply, 'No, our Lord. I swear by Thy name, I have never known what comfort is.' Afterwards another person will be brought who will have led a life of rank misery and misfortune on earth but will be found worthy of Paradise owing to his faithfulness to Allah and piety. He will be taken to Heaven and then led out of it immediately and asked, 'Have you ever known pain or misery?' 'No, our Lord!' he will reply, 'I swear by Thy name, I have never known what pain or misery is?' "

In truth, Allah has provided such wonderful joys and comforts in Paradise that a man who has passed his days in the world in utmost distress will forget all about it as soon as he has had a taste of them. Likewise, Hell is such an infernal place that a person who has lived all one's life in the world in rare luxury and happiness will at once, feel, on stepping into it, that he had never known what it was to be happy or comfortable.

The severity and dreadfulness of the chastisement of Hell can be imagined from this one hadiith (tradition) of the sacred Prophet (Peace be upon him):

"The mildest punishment that will be inflicted on a person in Hell is that he will be made to wear a pair of sandals made of fire which will be so hot as to set his brain boiling as if something was cooking in a pot on a stove."

The fare that will be served there has been indicated in the verses of the Qur-aan we have quoted already. Here, also, are two ahaadiith (traditions) of the Prophet (Peace be upon him):

"The stinking pus people will be made to drink in Hell is such that if a bucket of it was thrown into the world the whole world would be filled with its infernal stench."

"If a drop of zaqqum[1] were to fall on the earth, it would be enough to pollute all the articles of food and drink that are found here."

Brothers, — all the things the Glorious Qur-aan and the sacred Prophet (Peace be upon him) have told about the shape of things to come after death - the barzakh, the resurrection, the judgement and Heaven and Hell, that we have discussed here in this lesson and in the preceding one, are literally correct and true. There can be no doubting of them at all. By the Almighty, they will come to pass exactly as the Qur-aan and the august Prophet (Peace be upon him) have taught. We will see them ourselves, with our own eyes, after death.

The Last Day and Heaven and Hell have been dwelt upon in the Qur-aan and the ahaadiith (traditions) with such emphasis and thoroughness and referred to again and again a thousand times, for no other reason except to arouse in us a living, genuine anxiety to do all that lies in our power to save ourselves from the fearful penalty of Hell and attain the cherished, supremely delightful goal of Paradise.

Brothers, — life is transitory. One day we must die. Death is certain, and so is the Last Day. We will, surely, have to stand before Allah after death and answer for our deeds on earth. What, then, is our eternal home going to be — Heaven or Hell?

There is still time for us to mend our ways, to offer honest repentance for our misdeeds of the past and make a real, sincere effort for the attainment of Paradise.

Should, Allah forbid, the rest of our days in this world be also spent in neglect and folly, then, be sure, there is nothing in store for us in the hereafter save regret and the punishment of Hell.

O Allah we ask of You Jannah and that which brings towards it by word and deed and we seek refuge with You from the Fire and that which brings towards it by word and deed.

---

1. The infernal tree, mentioned in the Qur-aan, the fruit of which those doomed to the eternal punishment of Hell shall eat. — Translator.

Lesson 17

Dhikr

ISLAM STANDS FOR SELF-SURRENDER and submission to Allah. It calls on men to fashion their lives according to the Divine Will. It wants them to be loyal to Him in all circumstances and in every sphere of their conduct, personal as well as social. This can be possible only when our mind's eye is fixed permanently on the Almighty, and our consciousness of His love and Glory overshadows all our thoughts and actions.

It is, as such, one of the special teachings of Islaam that we remember Allah much and often and keep our tongues fresh with the recital of His Names, Praises and Attributes. It is an excellent and well-tried method for producing in our hearts His love and consciousness of His Greatness. It is natural for a man's heart to be filled with the love of anyone on whose splendour and excellence his mind dwells all the time.

In any way, it is a fact that frequent remembrance kindles the flame of love and lends strength to it and so also that the life of complete loyalty and submission to Allah which is the essence of Islaam can be possible only through Divine Love. It is love alone that makes one the willing bondsman of another. As a Persian verse says:

What is Love?

Say: To be the beloved's bondsman.

Consequently, very great stress has been laid in the Qur-aan and by the Prophet (Peace be upon him) on dhikr (Allahs remembrance). The Qur-aan reads:

"O ye who believe! celebrate the Praises of Allah, and do this often: and glorify Him morning and evening." — Surah Ahzaab (XXXIII), 41-42.

"And celebrate the Praises of Allah much and often: that ye may prosper." — Surah Jumu'ah (LXII), 10.

There are two things which lead one to forget Allah when one gets absorbed in them. These are wealth and family. So the Qur-aan names them specifically and warns Muslims against becoming a prisoner to them.

"O ye who believe! let not your riches or your children divert you from the remembrance of Allah. If any act thus, the loss is their own." — Surah *Munaafiquun (LXIII), 9.*

The five daily salaah (prayers) are obligatory for Muslims. These prayers, certainly, are a means of remembering Allah and a very good one too. But it would not be proper for a Muslim to stop at them, considering that if he had offered salaah he had done all that is required of him. When not in salaah one becomes unmindful and lax in the remembrance of Allah[1]. It is a clear commandment of Islaam that, in addition to salaah, one should also not neglect dhikr in whatever state one may be. It is said in Surah Nisaa:

"When ye pass (congregational) prayers, celebrate Allah's Praises standing, sitting down or lying down." — Surah *Nisaa (IV), 103.*

Thus, even those engaged in jihaad are enjoined to carry out the dhikr of Allah, keenly and enthusiastically. Says Surah Anfaal:

"O ye who believe! when ye meet a force, be firm and call Allah in remembrance much (and often); that ye may prosper." — Surah *Anfaal (VIII), 45.*

This verse, as the verse from Surah Jumu'ah we have quoted earlier, *"And celebrate the Praises of Allah much and often: That ye may prosper"*, shows that dhikr, by all means, constitutes an important factor in the success and felicity of the believers. As against it, the verse from Surah Munaafiquun we mentioned

---

1. It does not mean that, just as it is compulsory for a Muslim to offer salaah five times a day, in the same way it is essential for him to keep himself engaged always in the remembrance of Allah. What is required is that a Muslim should not be neglectful of the duty of remembering Allah.

earlier, candidly declares that those who neglect dhikr do a very wrong thing. They are at a great loss. In Surah Ra'd, further, it is stated as a characteristic of dhikr that it imparts peace and tranquility to the mind and the soul.

"For without doubt in the remembrance of Allah do hearts find satisfaction."
— Surah Ra'd (XIII), 28.

"It is related that once the Prophet (Peace be upon him) was asked who would be the most exalted among the servants of Allah on the Last Day. The Prophet (Peace be upon him) replied, 'Those who do the dhikr of Allah, be they men or women'."

Sayyidina Abu Musaa relates on the authority of the Prophet (Peace be upon him) that: "Those who remember Allah and those who do not are like those who are alive and those who are dead (i.e., those who remember Allah and celebrate His praises are alive while those who don't are dead)."

"Relates Sayyidina 'Abdullah bin 'Umar that the Prophet (Peace be upon him) once said, 'There is a polish for everything; for the hearts it is the dhikr of Allah. Nothing is more effective than dhikr for deliverance from divine chastisement'."

It should be understood clearly that the real meaning of dhikr is that a man should never be without the thought of Allah. In whatever circumstances he may be placed, with whatever thing he may be occupied, he must not allow himself to become unmindful of Allah, His laws and ordinances. Though for this it is not necessary that the tongue should also always be repeating His Names, Attributes etc. Such a state of permanent and all-pervading Allah-consciousness is commonly found only in devout bondsmen of the Lord who succeed in producing within themselves an everlasting awareness of Allah and a feeling of infinite devotion to Him through frequent dhikr. There is developing a tendency among some of the modern educated people to hold dhikr as futile. This is a grave folly. Dhikr is a most valuable instrument for forging a living and all-embracing link with Allah. The Prophet (Peace be upon him) was very clear about its worth and importance.

"It is related by Sayyidina 'Abdullah bin Busr that once a man presented himself before the Prophet (Peace be upon him) and said, 'O Prophet of Allah, there are numerous teachings of Islaam. Please tell me something which I may hold fast forever.' The Prophet (Peace be upon him) replied, 'Keep your tongue wet always with the dhikr (remembrance) of Allah'."

"Another hadiith (tradition) qudsii related by Sayyidina Abu Hurairah reads: Allah says, 'When anyone remembers Me and his lips move in My dhikr, I am by his side.' "

Some dhikr-formulas of the Prophet (Peace be upon him)

The value and importance of dhikr would have become apparent from the Qur-aanic verses and ahaadiith (traditions) we have just quoted. We have seen how dhikr of Allah promotes and strengthens Divine Love in our hearts. Below, we give some of the favourite dhikr-formulas of the noble Prophet (Peace be upon him).

Foremost

Relates Sayyidina Jaabir from the Prophet (Peace be upon him) that the best of all dhikrs is the dhikr of 'Laa ilaaha illallaah.'

Narrates Sayyidina Abu Hurairah that the Prophet (Peace be upon him) once remarked: "When anyone recites 'Laa ilaaha illallaah' from the depth of his heart, the gates of the heavens open for the kalimah till it reaches the seventh heaven and the 'Arsh, provided, of course, that the devotee abstains from the major sins."

According to another hadiith (tradition), the Prophet (Peace be upon him) is reported to have said, "Once Musaa (Moses) (Peace be upon him) begged the Lord to tell him something through which he could do His dhikr. The Lord told him to do so through the kalimah of 'Laa ilaaha illallaah', upon which Musaa (Moses) said, 'This is what everyone does. I want something special.' Came the reply, 'If the seven heavens and all the heavenly creatures and the seven climes on the earth and all that is contained in them are placed on one side of the balance (scale) and the kalimah of 'Laa ilaaha illallaah' on the other, the latter shall turn out to be heavier'."

Such, indeed, is the splendour of 'Laa ilaaha illallaah'. People, unfortunately, take it to be a mere phrase. The writer himself has heard it from an inspired devotee of the Lord in a moment of rare spiritual feeling that, "If someone with the entire wealth of the world at his command were to tell me to give him one kalimah of recited 'Laa ilaaha illallaah' by me in return for his treasures, this humble self shall refuse to do so."

The third kalimah

It is related by Sayyidina Samurah bin Jundub that the Prophet (Peace be upon him) once said that of all the spoken words and the kalimahs, the most excellent were these four:

$$سُبْحَانَ اللهِ وَالْحَمْدُ لِلّٰهِ وَلَا إِلٰهَ إِلَّا اللهُ وَاللهُ أَكْبَرْ$$

[Transliteration: Subhaa-nallaahi wal-hamdu lillaahi wa-laa ilaaha illal laahu wal-laahu akbar.]

Glory be to Allah and all praise be to Allah, and there is no deity (worthy of worship) save Allah, and Allah is Great.

Narrates Abu Hurairah that the Prophet (Peace be upon him) said, "The kalimah of 'Subhaa-nallaahi wal-hamdu lillaahi wa-laa ilaaha illal laahu wal-laahu akbar' is dearer to me than the entire world on which the sun shines'."

This kalimah is most complete and comprehensive and all the aspects of divine praise are covered by it. In some ahaadiith

99

(traditions) the phrase 'Laa howla walaa quwwata illaa billaah' is also included in it. It occurs after 'Allahu Akbar'. A revered spiritual mentor used to explain the importance of the kalimah to the writer in the following manner:

'Subhaa-nallaah.' 'Glory be to Allah.' — Free from all faults and blemishes and other things that are not worthy of His Glory.

'Alhamdu lillaah.' 'Praise be to Allah', He is the embodiment of perfection and the centre of every kind of virtue, (therefore) all praise is for Him, and when such is His Glory that He is absolutely blemishless and all the wonderful virtues are assembled in Him, He alone is our Lord and the sole object of our heart's desire.

'Laa ilaaha illallaah.' 'There is no deity (worthy of worship) save Allah.' — We are His own helpless slaves and of no one else.

'Allahu Akbar.' 'Allah is Great', — He is Most Powerful, Almighty. We can never acquit ourselves of our duties to Him as His slaves, nor can we ever gain nearness unto Him except that He Himself blesses us with His grace.

'Laa howla walaa quwwata illaa billaah.' 'There is no power or virtue but in Allah.'

Tasbiih Faatimii

A well-known hadiith (tradition) of the Prophet (Peace be upon him) has it that the Prophet's (Peace be upon him) beloved daughter (and Sayyidina 'Alii's wife), Sayyiditina Faatimah, used to perform all the domestic chores with her own hands. She had even to draw water from the well and to carry it home and to grind the corn in the millstone. One day she begged the noble Prophet (Peace be upon him) to provide her with a domestic servant upon which the Prophet (Peace be upon him) observed, "I will tell you of something that will serve you better than a domestic servant. Recite: 'Subhaa-nallaah' 33 times, 'Alhamdu lillaah' 33 times, and 'Allahu Akbar' 34 times after

100

each salaah and on retiring to bed. This will be of greater value to you than a servant.''

Another hadiith (tradition) says, ''Whoever will recite after each salaah 'Subhaa-nallaah' 33 times, 'Alhamdu lillaah' 33 times, and 'Allahu akbar' 34 times, and, at the end of it, the kalimah of 'Laa ilaaha illal laahu wahdahu laa sharika lahu lahul mulku wa-lahul hamdu wa-huwa 'alaa kulli shay-in qadiir.' ('There is no deity (worthy of worship) but one Allah. He is alone. No partner hath He. Unto Him belongs Sovereignty, and unto Him belongs Praise, and He is All-Powerful'), all his sins will be forgiven even if they be as profuse as the foam of the sea.''

Subhaa-nallaahi wa-bihamdi-hii

It is related by Sayyidina Abu Hurairah that the Prophet (Peace be upon him) said, ''He who will recite 'Subhaa-nallaahi wa-bihamdihi' a hundred times morning and evening regularly, no one shall take with him a greater provision of virtue to the hereafter than him, save the person who recited it even more.''

Another hadiith (tradition) related again by Sayyidina Abu Hurairah says: ''Two phrases sit very lightly on the tongue but are very heavy in the Balance (Scale) of Deeds and Allah loves them very much. These are: 'Subhaa-nallaahi wa-bi-hamdihi, subhaa-nallaahil 'adhiim'.''

There are many other dhikr-formulas commended by the Prophet (Peace be upon him). But the few we have given here are quite sufficient for anyone to adopt for regular recitation.

As regards the reward and recompense in the hereafter promised in the ahaadiith (traditions), it needs be noted that there is no fixed measure or a standard yardstick for it. Whoever will recite a kalimah of dhikr sincerely and with no other object than the propitiation of Allah will, In-Sha-Allah, merit the full reward, no matter how many

101

times and at what hour he does so. But when a spiritual guide prescribes a dhikr for anyone for a particular purpose, like the kindling of Divine Love, or the awakening of the heart and the creation of a permanent consciousness of Allah, or for the eradication of a moral or spiritual ailment, it is necessary to follow the routine he lays down and to do the dhikr as many times as he tells. Without this, the desired results cannot be obtained by the devotee. For example, if a person recites the Surah Faati-hah (Alhamdu lillaahi rabbil 'aala-miin) or any other surah of the Qur-aan as an act of religious merit, there is no harm if he does so once in the morning, once at noon, once in the afternoon, once in the evening and a couple of times in the night, but if he wants to learn the surah by heart, also, he will have to recite it scores of times during one sitting. Otherwise, he will not be able to memorise it. This is exactly the difference between an ordinary dhikr aimed only at Divine Reward, and the special dhikr which spiritual mentors prescribe to disciples for the cure of a spiritual morbidity or as a means for the attainment of any other objective of a similar category. Many people get caught in confusion because of not knowing this difference. This is why these few lines have been added here.

Reading of the Qur-aan[1].

The reading of the Qur-aan is also a very good dhikr: A hadiith (tradition) says:

"The superiority of the Word of Allah over any other word is the same as the superiority of Allah over any of His creatures."

---

1. Some people these days believe that mechanical reading of the Qur-aan, without following its meaning, is useless. They, perhaps, imagine the Qur-aan to be like any other book and just as it is futile to read a book unless one also understands what it says, in the same way they feel that reading of the Qur-aan also without following its import is meaningless. But the truth is that the Qur-aan is just not like any other book. It is the Book of Allah and nothing besides it. The mere reading of it, with

102

"And Sayyidina 'Abdullah bin Mas'ood relates on the authority of the Prophet (Peace be upon him) that, 'He who reads one letter of the Qur-aan, for him there is one virtue and the reward on this virtue is equal to that on ten other virtues. When I say this I do not mean that 'Alif-laam-miim' is one letter but that 'Alif' is one letter, 'Laam' another and 'Miim' the third.''

Yet another ha̲diit̲h̲ (tradition), as related by Sayyidina Abu Umaamah, reads:

"O People, read the Qur-aan. On the Day of Judgement the Qur-aan will intercede for those who will have been reading it (in their lives)."

Some suggestions

1. There is no need for those in whose hearts d̲hikr of Allah has come to dwell permanently as a result of constant endeavour and become a part of their existence, to follow a set routine or make a special effort in this respect. But if common people like us want to strengthen their bond with Allah and partake of its auspiciousness and blessedness, they must practise d̲hikr at a fixed time and in a fixed number

---

continued from previous page:

    due reverence and humility, is not without its significance. It indicates devotion to Allah, and, thus, becomes an act of worship. Had the purpose of reading the Qur-aan been only to realise its import and to appreciate intelligently what it seeks to convey, it would have been necessary to recite the Surah Faati-ha̲h as many as four times in the course of a single s̲alaah. Only once would have been enough for knowing its meaning. Such a misunderstanding arises, generally, among those who imagine Allah to be something of a worldly sovereign. They have no idea of His Supreme Belovedness and Worshipfulness. Their hearts do not fully participate in it. Together with this, it should also be remembered that the real purpose of the Qur-aan — guidance and instruction — can be realised only when it is properly understood, when it is read carefully and the meanings of its verses are studied diligently. This is the best way of reading it and a source of greater augustness. At the same time, the mere reading of the Qur-aan, also, is not futile. The correct and the balanced view in this matter is what we have stated here.

according to their individual circumstance. Better still, they should seek the advice of a spiritual guide while choosing a dhikr-formula for themselves. Or, they can select a kalimah from the kalimahs we have given above, which may be most suited to their temperament. Time should also be set aside daily for the recitation of the Qur-aan.

2. As far as possible the meaning of the kalimah used for dhikr should be kept in mind during recitation. The dhikr should be done with an active awareness of Divine Glory and Magnificence and with the feeling and the belief that Allah was near, right there, listening to every word that was being recited.

3. Wudu is not necessary for dhikr. It can be done freely without wudu. The reward will not suffer because of it. But the effulgence and spiritual effectiveness of dhikr is very much enhanced when it is done with wudu.

4. It has been seen earlier that the third kalimah 'Subhaa-nallaahi walhamdu lillaahi walaa ilaaha illallaahu wal-laahu akbar' is most comprehensive among all the kalimahs. If it is adopted for recitation, it can fulfil all the needs. This writer has seen that spiritual mentors generally prescribe it to their disciples along with durood shariif and istighfaar[1].

May Allah grant us the good fortune to fill our hearts and wet our tongues with dhikr, and favour us with the fruit of its illuminations and blessings.

---

1. Dealt with separately in Lessons 19 and 20.

Lesson 18

Du'aa

WHEN IT IS DEFINITE and beyond dispute that whatever happens in the world happens by the Will of Allah, and everything that exists lies absolutely in His power and control, it is manifestly natural for us to supplicate to Him in our needs, big as well as small. Followers of all religions beseech Allah and address their petitions to Him. But in Islaam it is a matter of paramount importance. States the Qur-aan:

"And your Lord says: Call on Me: I will answer (your prayer)." — Surah Mu-min (XL), 60.

"Say (to the rejectors): My Lord is not uneasy because of you if ye call not on Him." — Surah Furqaan (XXV), 77.

Together with calling on us to supplicate to the Lord in our needs, the Qur-aan also goes on to assure that He is very close to His servants. He hears their petitions and grants them.

"When My servants ask thee concerning Me, I am indeed close to them. I listen to the prayer of every supplicant when he calleth on Me." — Surah Baqarah (II), 186.

The noble Prophet (Peace be upon him) also assures that to beg to Allah for our needs, to turn to Him and to make our petitions to Him, is the very essence and marrow of worship. Says he:

"Du'aa (making of earnest entreaties to Allah) is worship." (According to another version, the <u>h</u>adii<u>th</u> (tradition) reads: "Du'aa is the essence and marrow of worship)."

"Nothing enjoys a loftier place in the sight of Allah than du'aa."

"Allah is displeased with those who do not beg for their needs to Him. The Prophet (Peace be upon him) is reported to have said, 'Allah is displeased with His servant who does not supplicate for his needs to Him'."

105

Glory be! If a person approaches a close friend or a near relative with his needs every now and then, they get sick of him, but Allah is so marvellously Gracious and Benevolent to His servants, that He gets angry if they do not turn to Him in their need. A hadiith (tradition) says:

"For whom the doors of du'aa have opened, for him the doors of mercy have opened."

Anyway, to pray to Allah for one's needs or for the realisation of one's ambitions, is not only a means to their fulfilment, but also a superb act of worship, and Allah is very happy with him who does so. He opens the gates of His mercy for him. This is true of all supplications, whether they be of a religious or spiritual nature or for a worldly need. The only condition is that the object or need should be of a lawful and legitimate kind. To pray for an improper or sinful thing is also improper and sinful.

The greater the depth of feeling, the stronger the realisation of one's own helplessness, and the firmer the conviction of Divine Omnipotence and Benevolence with which a prayer is made, the greater the chances are of its acceptance. A prayer which does not spring from the heart, but is uttered only by mouth as a formality, is not a prayer. The Prophet (Peace be upon him) says:

"Allah does not grant a prayer that is made with a sleeping heart."

Allah listens to prayers at all hours, but we learn from ahaadiith (traditions) that there are certain occasions on which, if a prayer is made, it stands greater chances of acceptance as, for instance, after a fard (obligatory) salaah, during the latter part of the night, at the time of breaking a fast, or at any other moment of a similar nature when a good act is performed, and during the course of a journey, particularly when it is undertaken for a religious purpose and for the sake of Allah.

It is not necessary for a man to be a saint, or innocent of sin, for his prayers to be granted. It is true that the prayers of noble and virtuous persons are granted more than those of others, but it does not mean

106

that the prayers of ordinary men and sinners are not heard at all. One, therefore, must not give up making supplications to Allah thinking what would the supplications of a sinner do. Allah, the Beneficent, the Merciful, listens to the prayers of His sinning servants, too, just as He feeds them and clothes them, in spite of their misdeeds. Everyone should, therefore, pray. We have seen how du'aa is a regular worship. Divine recompense will, in any case, be his who will engage himself in it.

It will be foolish to lose heart and cease praying if the object for which an earnest prayer is made to Allah is not realised. He, in any event, is not bound by our desires. Sometimes, in His judgement, it is in our own interest that our prayers should not be granted at once. Sometimes, delay is found by Him to be better for us. But, we, in our ignorance, get disheartened. We are inclined to be hasty and when our prayers are not answered we give up praying as futile. As a hadii_th (tradition) of the Prophet (Peace be upon him) assures us:

"Du'aa is never wasted, but the forms of its acceptance vary. Sometimes, a person gets what he begs for. Sometimes, Allah does not think it best for him that the thing he prays for should be granted. So, He does not give it to him but, in its place, a greater favour is bestowed on him, or an impending calamity is averted, or the prayer is made an atonement for sins. (Since the supplicant does not know it, he imagines that his entreaties and supplication have come to nothing). Sometimes, the prayer is turned into the harvest of the hereafter. The object for which a person prays is not granted to him in this life, but a greater reward is reserved for him in the life to come as a compensation thereof."

And, here is another:

"Some people, many of whose prayers had not been granted in this world, when they will see in the hereafter the glorious rewards and blessings that had been set aside for them as a recompense for the unfulfilled prayers, will exclaim sorrowfully how great would it have been had none of their prayers been granted in the world, so that they could get the compensation for them all in the hereafter."

To summarise, everyone who believes in Allah should make it a habit of his to call on Him for his needs with all his heart, and with an unshakeable faith in the Omnipotence and the Benevolence of the Almighty, and believing positively that the prayer will be granted. He must be sure in his heart that his prayer shall never, never go waste.

The endeavour should be to pray in words richly expressive of Divine Might and Magnificence and of one's own total helplessness. Many prayers are contained in the Qur-aan and hundreds of them in the ahaadiith (traditions) . These prayers, the prayers of the Qur-aan and the ahaadiith (traditions), are by far the best. A selection of forty one prayers is given at the end of the book.

Lesson 19

Durood Shariif

DUROOD SHARIIF IS AN INVOCATION we make to Allah to
bestow His choicest favours and blessings on the Prophet (Peace be
upon him). It is a kind of prayer. The truth is that, after Allah, the
greatest obligation on us is that of the sacred Prophet (Peace and
blessings of Allah be upon him). He underwent tremendous
hardships and endured the bitterest of persecutions in order to
convey the Divine Guidance to us. Had he not borne these trials and
sufferings, the light of Faith would never have reached us. We would
be dwelling in the gloom of apostasy and making our home in Hell
after death.

Since Faith is the greatest blessing on earth and we have attained
it solely through the merciful agency of the Prophet (Peace be upon
him), our greatest benefactor, next to Allah, is the Prophet
Muhammad (Peace be upon him). There is nothing we can do to
pay back the enormous debt of gratitude we owe him. We can only
pray for him to Allah as a token of our loyalty and gratefulness.

But what prayer can we make that may be worthy of the Prophet
(Peace be upon him)? Naturally, none, besides that Allah may
magnify him and bless him with His choicest favours. This is just
what durood is.

The Qur-aan clearly enjoins upon us to offer durood, and in what
a wonderful manner does it do so:

*"Allah and His angels send blessings on the Prophet : O Ye that believe!
send ye blessings on him and salute him with all respect."* — *Surah Ahzaab
(XXXIII), 56.*

In this verse we are first told that Allah Himself honours the
Prophet (Peace be upon him), and holds him in strongest affection,
and that His angels also do the same — they pay reverence to him
and beseech Allah to bless him with His most marvellous favours.

109

The verse then goes on to command us also, i.e., the believers to send blessings on him and salute him with all respect. Thus, before the command is given, care has been taken to explain to us that the thing we are being required to do, is something which is particularly pleasing to Allah and which the angels also fondly do. After knowing it, what Muslim is there worth his name who will not make it a religious duty to offer durood?

Below, we give a few ahaadiith (traditions) of the Prophet (Peace be upon him) extolling the virtue and merit of durood shariif.

The Prophet (Peace be upon him) is reported to have said: "He who will send blessings on me once, Allah will confer ten favours on him." (In another hadiith (tradition) it has also been said that, "Allah will forgive his ten sins and raise him higher in rank by ten degrees)."

"There are many angels of Allah whose special duty is that they keep on moving in the world, and whichever follower of mine sends blessings on me, they carry it to me at once."

Gracious is the Lord! Our durood is communicated to the Prophet (Peace be upon him) by the angels and through it we get a chance of being mentioned in his presence. What greater honour could there be for us, really?

The Prophet (Peace be upon him) says:

"Closest to me on the Day of Requital will be he who sends blessings on me oftener."

"That man is a big miser in whose presence my name is taken and he does not offer durood."

"May he be disgraced in whose presence my name is taken and he fails to offer durood."

In sum, to send blessings on the Prophet (Peace be upon him) is a foremost duty we owe to him, a source of stupendous virtue and blessedness and the fountainhead of prodigious blessings in this world and the next.

Words of durood

Once the Companions asked the Prophet (Peace be upon him), "How are we to offer durood and salutation?" The Prophet (Peace be upon him) advised them about Durood Ibraahiimii which is recited in salaah. We have already reproduced it in Lesson 2.

Very much similar to Durood Ibraahiimii, but a little shorter, is another durood which was also taught by the Prophet (Peace be upon him). It reads:

اَللَّهُمَّ صَلِّ عَلَى مُحَمَّدِنِ النَّبِيِّ الْأُمِّيِّ وَاَزْوَاجِهِ اُمَّهَاتِ الْمُؤْمِنِيْنَ وَذُرِّيَّتِهِ وَاَهْلِ بَيْتِهِ كَمَا صَلَّيْتَ عَلَى اِبْرَاهِيْمَ اِنَّكَ حَمِيْدُ مَّجِيْدُ .

[Transliteration: Allahumma salli 'alaa Muhammadi-nin nabiyyil ummi-yi wa-azwaajihii um-mahaatil mu-minii-na wa-dhur-riyyatihii wa-ahli baytihii kamaa sallayta 'alaa Ibraahiima innaka hamidum majiid.]

O Allah! magnify Prophet Muhammad, the Unlettered, his wives, the mothers of the faithful, his posterity (followers), and his family, as Thou hast magnified the family of Ibraahiim. Verily, Thou art the Praiseworthy, the Majestic.

Whenever we take the name of the Prophet (Peace be upon him) or talk about him or hear about him from anyone, we should at once send blessings on him. On such occasions it is enough to say only 'Sallallaahu 'alayhi wasallam' or, 'Alayhis salaatu wassa-laam'

Daily routine

Some determined persons with a natural flair and fondness for durood shariif make it a regular habit to recite it thousands of times daily. But if weak-willed men like ourselves can manage to recite it a hundred times, morning and evening, with proper devotion and reverence, they will profit so much by it and there will be such exquisite favours of the Prophet (Peace be upon him) on him, that it is not possible even to imagine them in this world.

The following durood shariif is suggested to those who may be wanting to know a brief one:

$$اَللّٰهُمَّ صَلِّ عَلٰى مُحَمَّدِنِ النَّبِيِّ الْاُمِّيِّ وَآلِهِ$$

[Transliteration: Allaahumma salli 'alaa Muhammad-nin nabiyyil ummiyyi wa-aa-lih.]

O Allah magnify Muhammad, the Unlettered Prophet, and his family.

Lesson 20

Taubah (repentance)

ALLAH HAS SENT DOWN HIS APOSTLES into the world and revealed His Books through them so that men may learn to distinguish good from evil, virtue from vice, and earn for themselves divine approbation and deliverance in the life to come, by abstaining from the wicked and the unlawful, and adopting what was good and virtuous. Thus, those who reject the Faith and refuse to believe in the Prophets and the Divine Guidance with which they had been raised up, their whole existence, so to speak, is one of defiance and transgression. They are totally indifferent to the message sent down by Allah. They will have nothing to do with it. Unless they believe in the messengers and apostles raised up by Allah and in the holy scriptures revealed by Him, and, particularly, in the Last of the Prophets, the Prophet Muhammad (Peace be upon him), and the Divine Book he brought, i.e., the Sacred Qur-aan, and accept his guidance, they can never hope to attain the good pleasure of Allah and success and salvation in the hereafter. The denial of Allah, His apostles and His Books, is not pardonable. It cannot be condoned. This fact has been made abundantly clear by every Prophet of Allah during his time. In any case, it is essential for the salvation of the apostates and polytheists that they first of all renounce apostasy and polytheism and take to the path of Faith and monotheism. Without it, salvation is not possible.

Those who believe in the prophets and affirm their intention to live according to their teachings also, sometimes, fall into error. They are misled by the devil or by their own base instincts or impulses into committing a sin. For such defaulters, Allah has kept the door of taubah (repentance) open.

Taubah means that if a person may slip into folly and be guilty of a sin or an act of transgression against the law of Allah, he should feel genuinely sorry and ashamed over it, and resolve sincerely not to do

113

so again, and seek the forgiveness of the Lord with all his heart. It is stated in the Qur-aan and the ahaadiith (traditions) that by doing only this much, a man's sin is forgiven and he succeeds in winning the pleasure of the Almighty.

It is essential to know that taubah (repentance) is not vocal penitence. It is not at all a matter of uttering so many words of repentance. The sorrow must be sincere, the shame must be felt in the heart and the resolution not to repeat the folly and be guilty of the sin again, must be totally genuine.

It is like this. Suppose in a fit of temper or in a moment of acute mental depression, a person swallows poison with the intention of killing himself. But when the poison begins to work and a thousand knives begin to tear his intestines into pieces and he knows that death is near, he repents his folly, and cries out in desperation for medical relief. Now, at that time, his first thought will be that if he survived he would never touch the poison again or think of committing suicide. This exactly should be the state of the man who repents after sin. His heart should be seized with the fear of Divine Chastisement, the resolution not to do the thing again should be an honest resolution and so also his entreaties to Allah for forgiveness.

If such a state of feeling is realised by a person in any degree, he should be sure that the stain of sin has been washed away and the gates of mercy have opened for him. After such a taubah the sinner is completely absolved of his sin, he is thoroughly sanctified and becomes even dearer in the sight of Allah than he was before, so much so that, sometimes, a person succeeds in attaining, through taubah, a place which would be hard to reach even after a hundred years of prayer and fasting.

All that we have said on the subject of taubah was derived entirely from the twin sources of the Qur-aan and the ahaadiith (traditions). We are now going to consider some of the relevant verses of the Qur-aan:

"O ye who believe! turn to Allah with sincere repentance: in the hope that your Lord will remove from you your ills and admit you to Gardens beneath which rivers flow." — Surah Taḥriim (LXVI), 8.

"Why turn they not to Allah, and seek his forgiveness? For Allah is Oft-Forgiving, Most Merciful." — Surah Maa-i-dah (V), 74.

"When those come to thee who believe in our signs: 'Peace be on you! your Lord hath inscribed for Himself (the rule of) Mercy. Verily, If any of you did evil in ignorance, and thereafter repented, and amended (his conduct); Lo, He is Oft-Forgiving, Most Merciful'." — Surah An'aam (VI), 54.

Also, look at the following aḥaadiith (traditions):

"Allah says, 'O My creatures! you commit follies day and night and I can forgive them all. So, seek My forgiveness. I will forgive'."

"Allah extends the arm of Mercy and Forgiveness every night so that the sinners of the day may repent and seek His pardon, and every day so that the sinners of the night may repent and seek His pardon, and it shall be like this with Allah till the sun rises from the west near the Doomsday."

"A man committed a sin, and, then, he prayed to Allah, 'O Lord, I have sinned. Forgive me.' Upon this, the Lord observed, 'My servant knows that there is an Allah who can punish him for his sin as well as forgive. I have forgiven the sin of My servant.' The person abstained from sin as long as the Lord wished, after which he again went astray and fell into transgression. He, once again, prayed to Allah, 'O Lord, I have sinned. Forgive me.' The Lord observed, 'My servant knows that there is an Allah who can chastise him for sinning as well as forgive. I have forgiven the sin of My servant.' He remained free from sin as long as the Lord wished, and, then was, again, guilty of it. Once again he prayed to Allah, 'O Lord, I have sinned. Forgive me.' The Lord observed, 'My servant knows for certain that there is an Allah who can punish as well as forgive him for his sin. I have forgiven the sin of My servant'."

115

"One who seeks divine forgiveness after sin becomes like one who has never been guilty of sin."

These ahaadiith (traditions) show how Merciful and Oft-Forgiving is the Lord. To get emboldened by them and to start indulging freely in sinful activities on the strength of taubah (repentance), is not worthy of a Muslim. Such verses and ahaadiith (traditions) should, on the contrary, lend greater strength to the love of Allah. They should make one feel that it really was the height of meanness to act against the wishes of such a Compassionate and Benevolent Lord. If a master be of most kind and affectionate nature, would it behove His servants to pay back His kindness and affection by violating His wishes, by disobeying His commands?

What these verses and ahaadiith (traditions) seek to convey, is that should a person succumb to the temptations of the devil or to his own ignoble desires and inclinations and commit a sin, he must not despair of the mercy of the Lord and lose all hope of salvation. He should, on the other hand, turn his back immediately on the lapse and try earnestly to remove its stain through taubah, by begging Allah, in all sincerity, for His forgiveness. The Almighty, in His Infinite Mercy, will forgive, and instead of being angry with the sinner, He will become even more pleased for regretting sincerely what he had done and turning to Him hopefully for remission. A hadiith (tradition) states:

"When a man turns to Allah after sin and repents sincerely for his folly, it makes Allah even happier than a rider whose mount may have thrown him down in a vast desert and fled away with all the journey's provisions laden on its back, and, when the rider may have resigned himself to his fate and sat down under a tree to wait for his death, the animal may return all of a sudden, with the provisions intact and the rider may catch hold of it and blurt out (stupidly) in sheer joy, 'O Allah, Thou, indeed, art my slave and me Thy Master'."

If, after knowing these verses and ahaadiith (traditions), someone still fails to seek divine forgiveness and approbation by offering repentance for his sins through taubah and resolving not to fall into error again, he, emphatically, is most unfortunate.

Many people are inclined to take a most complacent attitude towards taubah. They say, "We are healthy and strong, so what's the hurry? We will do taubah before dying." Brothers, this is an extremely dangerous deception which the devil practices on us. Deprived as he has himself of Divine Mercy and Beneficence and earned a permanent abode in Hell, he wants us also to go his way. No one knows when death may strike. Thus, we should consider each day to be the last day of our lives and lose no time in begging the forgiveness of Allah, if and when we have been guilty of an evil. This, alone, is the path of wisdom. It is stated candidly in the Qur-aan that:

"Allah accepts the repentance of those who do evil in ignorance and repent soon afterwards; to them will Allah turn in mercy; for Allah is full of knowledge and wisdom. Of no effect is the repentance of those who continue to do evil, until death faces one of them, and he says, 'Now have I repented indeed!' Nor of those who die rejecting faith: for them have We prepared a punishment most grievous." — Surah Nisaa (IV), 17-18.

We should catch time by the forelock and realise the value of life that is left to us. We should not put off taubah by a moment; we must not procrastinate. We ought to set about, at once, reforming our ways. Allah alone knows when death is going to make its call on us, and, then, it may be too late. Who can tell whether, at that time, we will get the opportunity to offer taubah or not?

Brothers, — we all have seen people dying. The general experience is that a person dies in the same state in which he has led his life. It does not normally happen that a person may have spent all his days in folly and negligence, and, then, suddenly repented and turned into a saint a day or two before his death. Hence, a man who wants to die in a state of piety, for him it is necessary to become pious in his lifetime. Then alone, can he hope to die as a good Muslim by the grace of Allah, and to be raised up with the faithful and the righteous in the hereafter.

117

If, after offering repentance for a sin, a person may be guilty of the same sin again, there is no need for him to feel so frustrated over it as to lose faith in Divine Mercifulness. He should offer taubah quickly again, and if again he may break it, he should not hesitate to offer it once more, even if it be a thousand times. Whenever he will repent with a sincere heart, it is the promise of Allah that He will accept his repentance and forgive him. The Benevolence of the Lord, like His Paradise, is infinite.

Words of taubah

From the foregoing it would have been clear that in whatever words or language a person may offer taubah, Allah will listen and accept his penitence. But the noble Prophet (Peace be upon him) has laid down certain specific phrases or prayers in this regard which he used to recite himself. These prayers surely, are most auspicious, most worthy of His acceptance and most pleasing to Him. We are reproducing some of these here for you to learn by heart and recite for seeking Divine Forgiveness.

اَسْتَغْفِرُ اللّٰهَ الَّذِيْ لَا اِلٰهَ اِلَّا هُوَ الْحَيُّ الْقَيُّوْمُ وَاَتُوْبُ اِلَيْهِ

[Transliteration: Astagh-firullaa-hal ladhii laa ilaaha illaa huwal hayyul qayyumu wa-a-tubu ilayhi.]

I beg the forgiveness of Allah, save Whom there is no deity (worthy of worship), the Living, the Eternal. Unto Him do I turn penitent.

The Prophet (Peace be upon him) has said, "Whoever will offer penitence to Allah and implore His forgiveness through this kalimah, Allah will forgive him, even if he has fled from the field of jihaad, which is a most mortal sin in the sight of Allah."

And again: "Whoever will recite this kalimah thrice before going to sleep, Allah will forgive his sins, even though they may be as profuse as the foam of the sea'. "

118

Sometimes the sacred Prophet (Peace be upon him) used to recite only 'Astagh-firullaah'. (I implore the forgiveness of the Lord). It is a very brief phrase and we should try to cultivate the habit of repeating it every now and then.

Sayyidul Istighfaar

It is related that the noble Prophet (Peace be upon him) once remarked that the following prayer is Sayyidul Istighfaar (the leader of all the prayer-formulas of repentance).

اَللّٰهُمَّ اَنْتَ رَبِّيْ لَا اِلٰهَ اِلَّا اَنْتَ خَلَقْتَنِيْ وَاَنَا عَبْدُكَ وَاَنَا عَلٰى عَهْدِكَ وَوَعْدِكَ مَا اسْتَطَعْتُ ، اَعُوْذُ بِكَ مِنْ شَرِّ مَا صَنَعْتُ ، اَبُوْءُ لَكَ بِنِعْمَتِكَ عَلَيَّ وَاَبُوْءُ بِذَنْبِيْ ، فَاغْفِرْ لِيْ فَاِنَّهُ لَا يَغْفِرُ الذُّنُوبَ اِلَّا اَنْتَ

[Transliteration: Allahumma anta rabbi laa ilaaha illaa anta, kha-laqtanii wa-ana 'abduka wa-ana 'alaa ah-dika wa-wa'dika masta-ta'tu, a-'oodhu bika min sharri maa sa-na'tu, a-bu-oo laka bini'matika 'alayya, wa-a-buu-oo bi-dhambii fagh-firlii fa-innahu laa yagh-firudh dhunuba illaa anta.]

O Allah! Thou art my Lord. There is no deity save Thee. Thou art my Creator and I am Thy slave. I abide by Thy covenant and promise as best as I can. I seek refuge in Thee from the mischief of what I have wrought. I acknowledge unto Thee Thy favour which Thou hast bestowed upon me. I also confess my inequity; so forgive me for none forgiveth sins save Thee.

Says the Prophet (Peace be upon him):

"He who will offer repentance and beg the forgiveness of Allah by reciting this prayer with faith and sincerity during daytime, then if he died on that day, before nightfall, he shall go to Heaven, and he who will recite it at night, before daybreak, he shall go to Heaven."

The three kalimahs of taubah we have mentioned above are quite easy to remember.

As a hadiith (tradition) reads:

"Blessed, indeed, is the man in whose record the profusion of taubah is written."

Another hadiith states:

The Prophet (Peace be upon him) said: "The bondsman that holds onto taubah (repents to Allah from sins constantly), Allah will save him from all difficulties; remove all his hardships and sorrow; and grant him sustenance from such a source which he cannot imagine."

Epilogue

WHAT HAS BEEN STATED in the twenty lessons of this small volume will, In-Sha-Allah (If Allah Wills), suffice for anyone for the attainment of Divine Pleasure and Paradise. It seems appropriate here to give a brief resume of the whole discussion before bringing the book to a close.

The first principle of Islaam and the most essential pre-requisite of deliverance and the attainment of Paradise, is that a man affirms his faith in the kalimah of 'Laa ilaaha illallaah Muhammadur rasu-lullaah' After this, he should try to acquire knowledge of the tenets of Islaam, at least as far as it is necessary to know them in order to be a good Muslim. His constant endeavour should be to observe the Islaamic teachings faithfully, and carry out sincerely the Divine Commandments regarding the Rights of Allah, as well as the Rights of Man and good social and moral behaviour. When there may occur a lapse on his part in respect of these matters, he should feel genuinely sorry over it and repent to Allah and seek His forgiveness. He should resolve honestly not to be guilty of the transgression again. If he has transgressed against a fellow being by violating his rights or doing him any other harm, he should seek his pardon and make amends for his fault and misconduct, or pay suitable compensation as the case may be.

In the same way, the effort of a Muslim should always be that the love of Allah and His Apostle and Faith should be stronger in His heart than that of anyone or anything else in the world. He should remain steadfast in Faith and waver not in the least from the path of duty to Allah and the Prophet (Peace be upon him), whatever the circumstances. He should, also, as a matter of duty, take some part in the preaching and propagation of Islaam. It is some thing of outstanding virtue and merit and a most special legacy of the Prophets. In the present age, particularly, its value is much greater than that of all other supererogatory prayers and forms of worship, and when a person devotes himself to it, his devotion to Allah, the Prophet and Faith, also develops and becomes stronger.

Among the supererogatory prayers, if possible, one should develop the habit of tahajjud (voluntary prayers performed in the latter part of the night). Its auspiciousness is of the very highest category.

One must always be on one's guard against sin, specially against the major sins, like adultery, stealing, falsehood, drinking alcohol, and dishonesty in monetary affairs.

It is advisable to do some dhikr every day. In case it may not be possible to spare more time for it, one should recite at least Kalimah Tamjid[1] or only 'Subhaa-nallaahi wa-bihamdihi' and istighfaar[2] and durood shariif[3], a hundred times each, morning and evening.

Time should also be set aside for the daily reading of the Qur-aan. It should be done with due religious respect and reverence. After every obligatory salaah and at bedtime, Tasbiih Faatimii[4] may also be recited.

For those who aspire for more, the advice is to seek guidance from a spiritual mentor who may be worthy of it. The last thing to be said in this connection is that the company of true, pious and exalted devotees of Allah and attachment and devotion to them, is the very elixir of religious and spiritual existence. If this can fall to the lot of anyone, all the rest will follow automatically.

---

1. 'Subhaa-nallaahi wal-hamdu lillaahi walaa ilaaha illallaahu wallaahu akbar.'
2. 'Astaghfirullaahal ladhii laa ilaaha illaa huwal hayyul qayyumu wa-atu-bu ilayhi', or only 'Astaghfirullaah', 'Astaghfirullaah'.
3. Durood Ibraahiimii or a brief one like 'Allahumma salli 'alaa sayyidinaa Muhammadi-nin nabiyyil ummiyyi wa-aa-lihi.'
4. 'Subhaa-nallaah' 33 times, 'Alhamdu lillaah' 33 times, 'Allahu Akbar' 34 times.

Appendix I.

Prayers from the Qur-aan and the aḥaadii<u>th</u> (traditions):

BELOW WE GIVE A SELECTION of forty one prayers from the Qur-aan and the aḥaadii<u>th</u> (traditions) as indicated in Lesson 17.

1.

اَلْحَمْدُ لِلّٰهِ رَبِّ الْعَالَمِيْنَ ٥ اَلرَّحْمٰنِ الرَّحِيْمِ ٥ مَالِكِ يَوْمِ الدِّيْنِ ٥ اِيَّاكَ نَعْبُدُ وَاِيَّاكَ نَسْتَعِيْنُ ٥ اِهْدِنَا الصِّرَاطَ الْمُسْتَقِيْمَ ٥ صِرَاطَ الَّذِيْنَ اَنْعَمْتَ عَلَيْهِمْ ٥ غَيْرِ الْمَغْضُوْبِ عَلَيْهِمْ وَلَا الضَّالِّيْنَ ٥

آمِيْن

[Transliteration: Alḥamdu lillaahi rabbil 'aa-lamiin, ar-raḥmaanir ra-ḥiim, maaliki yau-mid diin, iyyaaka na'budu wa-iyyaaka nasta'iin, ihdinas ṣi-raaṭal mustaqiim, ṣi-raaṭal la<u>dh</u>ii-na 'an-amta 'alayhim, <u>gh</u>ayril ma<u>gh</u>-dubi 'alayhim wala<u>d</u> <u>d</u>aulliin. Aa-miin.

Praise be to Allah, Lord of the Worlds, the Compassionate, the Merciful, Owner of the Day of Judgement. Thee alone do we worship, and to Thee alone do we beg for help. Show us the straight path; the path of those whom Thou hast favoured; not the path (of those) who earn Thine anger, nor of those who go astray. Aa-miin! — Surah Faati-ḥah, 1 - 7.

2.

رَبَّنَا آتِنَا فِي الدُّنْيَا حَسَنَةً وَّفِي الْاٰخِرَةِ حَسَنَةً وَّقِنَا عَذَابَ النَّارِ ·

[Transliteration: Rabbanaa aa-tinaa fiddunyaa ḥasanataw wa-fil-aa-<u>kh</u>i-rati ḥasanataw wa-qinaa a-<u>dh</u>aaban naar.]

Our Lord! Give us good in this world and good in the hereafter, and defend us from the torment of the Fire. — Surah Baqarah, 201.

123

3.

رَبَّنَا اِنَّنَا آمَنَّا فَاغْفِرْ لَنَا ذُنُوْبَنَا وَقِنَا عَذَابَ النَّارِ .

[Transliteration: Rabbanaa in-na-naa aa-mannaa, fagh-fir lanaa dhu-nuu-banaa wa-qinaa 'a-dhaa-ban naar.]

Our Lord! We have, indeed believed; forgive us then, our sins, and save us from the agony of the Fire. — Surah Aali 'Imraan, 16.

4.

رَبَّنَا اغْفِرْ لَنَا ذُنُوْبَنَا وَاِسْرَافَنَا فِيْ اَمْرِنَا وَثَبِّتْ اَقْدَامَنَا وَانْصُرْنَا عَلَى الْقَوْمِ الْكَافِرِيْنَ .

[Transliteration: Rabbanagh-fir lanaa dhu-nuu-banaa wa-israa-fanaa fii amrinaa wa-thabbit aqdaa-manaa wan-surnaa 'a-lal qaumil kaa-firiin.]

O Lord! Forgive us our sins and anything we may have done that transgressed our duty, establish our feet firmly, and help us against those people that resisteth Faith. — Surah Aali 'Imraan, 147.

5.

رَبَّنَا اِنَّنَا سَمِعْنَا مُنَادِيًا يُّنَادِيْ لِلْاِيْمَانِ اَنْ آمِنُوْا بِرَبِّكُمْ فَآمَنَّا ،
رَبَّنَا فَاغْفِرْ لَنَا ذُنُوْبَنَا وَكَفِّرْ عَنَّا سَيِّئَاتِنَا وَتَوَفَّنَا مَعَ الْاَبْرَارِ ،
رَبَّنَا وَآتِنَا مَا وَعَدْتَنَا عَلَى رُسُلِكَ وَلَا تُخْزِنَا يَوْمَ الْقِيَامَةِ اِنَّكَ لَا تُخْلِفُ الْمِيْعَادَ .

[Transliteration: Rabbanaa in-na-naa sami'naa munaa-di-yay yu-naadi lil-imaani an aa-minuu bi-rabbikum fa-aa-mannaa. Rabbanaa fagh-fir la-naa dhu-nuu-banaa wa-kaf-fir 'an-naa sayyi-aa-tinaa wa-ta-waffanaa ma'al abraar. Rabbanaa wa-aa-tinaa maa wa-'ad-tanaa 'a-laa rusu-lika wa-laa tukh-zinaa yaumal qiyaamati in-naka laa tukh-liful mii'aad.]

Our Lord! We have heard the call of one calling us to Faith, "Believe ye in the Lord", and we have believed. Our Lord! forgive us our sins, blot out from us our inequities and take to Thyself our souls in the company of the righteous. Our Lord! grant us what Thou didst promise unto us through Thine Apostle, and save us from shame on the Day of Judgement: for Thou never breakest Thy promise. — Surah Aali 'Imraan, 193 - 194.

6.

رَبَّنَا ظَلَمْنَا اَنْفُسَنَا وَاِن لَّمْ تَغْفِرْ لَنَا وَتَرْحَمْنَا لَنَكُونَنَّ مِنَ الْخَاسِرِيْنَ .

[Transliteration: Rabba-naa zalam-naa anfu-sa-naa wa-illam tagh-fir lanaa wa-tar-ham-naa la-na-kuu-nan-na minal khaa-si-riin.]

Our Lord! We have wronged our souls; if Thou forgive us not and bestow not on us Thy mercy, we shall certainly be lost. — Surah Aa'raaf, 23.

7.

رَبَّنَا لَا تَجْعَلْنَا فِتْنَةً لِّلْقَوْمِ الظَّالِمِيْنَ ، وَنَجِّنَا بِرَحْمَتِكَ مِنَ الْقَوْمِ الْكَافِرِيْنَ .

[Transliteration: Rabba-naa laa taj'alnaa fit-natal lil-qau-miz zaa-limiin, wa-najji-naa bi-rah-matika minal qaumil kaa-firiin.]

Our Lord! Make us not a trial for those who practise oppression, and deliver us by Thy mercy from those who reject Thee. — Surah Yuunus, 85 - 86.

8.

فَاطِرَ السَّمٰوٰتِ وَالْاَرْضِ ، اَنْتَ وَلِيِّيْ فِي الدُّنْيَا وَالْآخِرَةِ ، تَوَفَّنِيْ مُسْلِمًا وَّاَلْحِقْنِيْ بِالصَّالِحِيْنَ .

[Transliteration: Faa-tiras samaa-waati wal-ardi, an-ta waliy-yii
fid-dunyaa wal-aa-khi-rah, ta-waf-fanii musli-maw wa-alhiq-nii
bis-saa-li-hiin.]

*Creator of the heavens and the earth! Thou art my Protector in this
world and the hereafter. Take Thou my soul at death as one
submitting to Thy Will (as a Muslim), and unite us with the righteous.
— Surah Yuusuf, 101.*

9.

رِبِّ اجْعَلْنِيْ مُقِيْمَ الصَّلٰوةِ وَمِنْ ذُرِّيَّتِيْ رَبَّنَا وَتَقَبَّلْ دُعَاءِ ،
رَبَّنَا اغْفِرْ لِيْ وَلِوَالِدَيَّ وَلِلْمُؤْمِنِيْنَ يَوْمَ يَقُوْمُ الْحِسَابُ .

[Transliteration: Rabbij'al-nii muqii-mas-salaati wa-min dhur-riyyatii
rabbanaa wa-ta-qabbal du'aa, rabba-nagh-fir-lii wa-li-waa-li-dayya
wa-lil mu-minii-na yauma yaquu-mul hisaab.]

*O my Lord! Make me one who establishes regular prayer, and also raise
among my offspring, O our Lord, and accept Thou my prayer. O our Lord!
cover us with Thy forgiveness — me, my parents and all believers, on the
Day that the Reckoning will be established. — Surah Ibraahiim, 40 - 41.*

10.

رَبِّ ارْحَمْهُمَا كَمَا رَبَّيَانِيْ صَغِيْرًا .

[Transliteration: Rabbir-ham-humaa kamaa rabba-yaa-nii saghii-raa.]

*My Lord! Bestow on my parents Thy mercy even as they cherished me in my
childhood. — Surah Israa [Banii Israa-eel], 24.*

11.

رَبِّ زِدْنِيْ عِلْمًا .

[Transliteration: Rabbi zidnii 'ilman.]

O my Lord! Advance me in my knowledge. — Surah Taa-Haa, 114.

12.

رَبِّ اغْفِرْ وَارْحَمْ وَأَنْتَ خَيْرُ الرَّاحِمِينَ

[Transliteration: Rabbigh-fir war-ham wa-an-ta khayrur raahi-miin.]

O my Lord! Grant Thou forgiveness and mercy! For Thou art the Best of those who show mercy. — Surah Mu-minuun, 118.

13.

رَبِّ اَوْزِعْنِيْ اَنْ اَشْكُرَ نِعْمَتَكَ الَّتِيْ اَنْعَمْتَ عَلَيَّ وَعَلَى وَالِدَيَّ وَاَنْ اَعْمَلَ صَالِحًا تَرْضٰهُ وَاَصْلِحْ لِيْ فِيْ ذُرِّيَّتِيْ ، اِنِّيْ تُبْتُ اِلَيْكَ وَاِنِّيْ مِنَ الْمُسْلِمِيْنَ .

[Transliteration: Rabbi ow-zi'nii an ash-kura ni'ma-takal latii an'am-ta 'a-layya wa-'alaa waa-li-dayya wa-an aa'mala saali-han tar-daa-hu wa-as-lih-lii fii dhur-riyyatii, innii tubtu ilayka wa-innii minal muslimiin.]

O my Lord! Grant me that I may be grateful for Thy favour which Thou hast bestowed upon me, and upon both my parents, and I may work righteousness such as Thou mayst approve; and be gracious to me in my offspring. Truly I have turned to Thee, and truly I am from the Muslims. — Surah Ahqaaf, 15.

14.

رَبَّنَا اغْفِرْ لَنَا وَلِاِخْوَانِنَا الَّذِيْنَ سَبَقُوْنَا بِالْاِيْمَانِ وَلَا تَجْعَلْ فِيْ قُلُوْبِنَا غِلًّا لِّلَّذِيْنَ آمَنُوْا رَبَّنَا اِنَّكَ رَءُوْفٌ رَّحِيْمٌ .

[Transliteration: Rabba-nagh-fir lanaa wa-li-ikh-waa-ninal ladhii-na saba-quunaa bil-imaani wa-laa taj'al fii quluu-binaa ghil-lal lil-ladhii-na aa-manuu rabbanaa innaka ra-oo-fur rahiim.]

127

Our Lord! Forgive us, and our brethren who came before us into the Faith, and leave not, in our hearts, rancour (or sense of injury) against those who have believed. Our Lord! Thou art indeed, full of kindness, Most Merciful. — Surah Hashr, 10.

15.

رَبَّنَا اَتْمِمْ لَنَا نُوْرَنَا وَاغْفِرْ لَنَا ، اِنَّكَ عَلَى كُلِّ شَيْءٍ قَدِيْرٌ

[Transliteration: Rabbanaa atmim lanaa nu-ranaa wagh-fir lanaa, innaka 'a-laa kulli shay-in qadiir.]

Our Lord! Perfect our Light for us and grant us forgiveness, for Thou hast power over all things. — Surah Tahriim, 8.

16.

يَا حَيُّ يَا قَيُّوْمُ بِرَحْمَتِكَ اَسْتَغِيْثُ ، اَصْلِحْ لِيْ شَأْنِيْ كُلَّهُ

[Transliteration: Yaa hayyu yaa qayyuu-mu bi-rahmatika asta-ghiith, aslih lii sha-nii kullah.]

O Thou Living, Eternal One! Unto Thy Mercy do I appeal. Set aright all my states and all my deeds.

17.

اَللّٰهُمَّ اَصْلِحْ لِيْ دِيْنِيَ الَّذِيْ هُوَ عِصْمَةُ اَمْرِيْ ، وَاَصْلِحْ لِيْ دُنْيَايَ الَّتِيْ فِيْهَا مَعَاشِيْ ، وَاَصْلِحْ لِيْ آخِرَتِيَ الَّتِيْ فِيْهَا مَعَادِيْ ، وَاجْعَلِ الْحَيَاةَ زِيَادَةً لِّيْ فِيْ كُلِّ خَيْرٍ ، وَاجْعَلِ الْمَوْتَ رَاحَةً لِّيْ مِنْ كُلِّ شَرٍّ

[Transliteration: Alla-hummas-lih lii dii-niyal ladhii huwa 'is-matu amrii, was-lih lii dun-yaa-yal latii fiihaa ma-'aa-shii, was-lih lii aa-khi-rati-yal latii fii-haa ma'aa-dii, waj'a-lil hayaa-ta ziyaa-datal lii fii kulli khay-rin, waj'a-lil mauta raa-ha-tal lii min kulli sharr.]

O Allah! Set aright my faith which is the safeguard of all my affairs; set aright my world wherein is my living; set aright my hereafter whereto I have to return. Let life be unto me a source of advance in every kind of righteousness, and let death be to me a release from every kind of evil.

18.

اَللّٰهُمَّ اِنِّيْ اَسْأَلُكَ الْعَفْوَ وَالْعَافِيَةَ فِي الدُّنْيَا وَالْاٰخِرَةِ

[Transliteration: Allaa-humma innii as-a-lukal 'af-wa wal-'aa-fiya-ta fid-dunyaa wal-aa-khi-rah.]

O Allah! I beg of Thee forgiveness and peace in this world and the next.

19.

اَللّٰهُمَّ اِنِّيْ اَسْأَلُكَ الْهُدٰى وَالتُّقٰى وَالْعَفَافَ وَالْغِنٰى

[Transliteration: Allaa-humma innii as-a-lukal hudaa wat-tuqaa wal-'a-faa-fa wal-ghi-naa.]

O Allah! I beg of Thee guidance and modesty and righteousness and freedom from want.

20.

اَللّٰهُمَّ اِنِّيْ اَسْأَلُكَ رِزْقًا طَيِّبًا وَّعِلْمًا نَّافِعًا وَّعَمَلًا مُّتَقَبَّلًا

[Transliteration: Allaa-humma innii as-a-luka rizqan tayyibaw wa'ilman naa-fi'aw wa'ama-lam muta-qabbalan.]

O Allah! I beg of Thee sustenance that is clean; knowledge that is useful; and conduct that is acceptable to Thee.

21.

اَللَّهُمَّ افْتَحْ لِيْ اَبْوَابَ رَحْمَتِكَ وَسَهِّلْ لِيْ اَبْوَابَ رِزْقِكَ

[Transliteration: Allaa-hummaf-tah lii ab-waaba rah-matika wa-sahhil lii ab-waaba riz-qik.]

O Allah! Open the doors of Thy Mercy for me and make easy for me the doors of sustenance.

22.

اَللَّهُمَّ اكْفِنِيْ بِحَلَالِكَ عَنْ حَرَامِكَ وَاغْنِنِيْ بِفَضْلِكَ عَمَّنْ سِوَاكَ

[Transliteration: Allaa-hummak fi-nii bi-halaa-lika 'an haraa-mika wagh-ninii bi-fad-lika 'am-man siwaak.]

O Allah! Let Thy lawful sustenance suffice for me against unlawful sustenance, and let me be, by Thy Grace, dependant on no one besides Thee.

23.

اَللَّهُمَّ وَفِّقْنِيْ لِمَا تُحِبُّ وَتَرْضٰى ، وَاجْعَلْ آخِرَتِيْ خَيْرًا مِّنَ الْأُوْلٰى

[Transliteration: Allaa-humma waf-fiqnii limaa tu-hibbu wa-tar-daa, waj'al aa-khi-ra-tii khay-ram minal oo-laa.]

O Allah! Let it be my good fortune to do things that are pleasing to Thee and make the hereafter better for me than this world.

24.

اَللَّهُمَّ اَلْهِمْنِيْ رُشْدِيْ وَقِنِيْ شَرَّ نَفْسِيْ

[Transliteration: Allaa-humma al-him-nii rush-dii wa-qinii shar-ra naf-sii.]

130

O Allah! Guide me to the right path, to the path of truth and piety, and save me from the mischief of my own self.

25.

اَللّٰهُمَّ اَعِنِّيْ عَلٰى ذِكْرِكَ وَشُكْرِكَ وَحُسْنِ عِبَادَتِكَ

[Transliteration: Allaa-humma 'a-innii 'alaa dhik-rika wa-shuk-rika wa-husni 'i-baa-da-tik.]

O Allah! Help me in Thy remembrance and in being thankful to Thee and in good worship.

26.

يَا مُقَلِّبَ الْقُلُوبِ ثَبِّتْ قَلْبِيْ عَلٰى دِيْنِكَ

[Transliteration: Yaa mu-qal-libal quluubi thabbit qalbii 'a-laa dii-nik.]

O Thou who controlleth the hearts! Keep my heart steadfast in Thy faith.

27.

اَللّٰهُمَّ اَحْيِنِيْ مُسْلِمًا وَّأَمِتْنِيْ مُسْلِمًا

[Transliteration: Allaa-humma ah-yi-nii muslimaw wa-a-mitnii musliman.]

O Allah! Grant me that I may live as a Muslim and die as a Muslim.

28.

اَللّٰهُمَّ اِنِّيْ اَسْأَلُكَ حُبَّكَ وَحُبَّ مَن يُّحِبُّكَ وحُبَّ عَمَلٍ يُقَرِّبُ اِلٰى حُبِّكَ ، اَللّٰهُمَّ اجْعَلْ حُبَّكَ اَحَبَّ اِلَيَّ مِنْ نَفْسِيْ وَمِنْ اَهْلِيْ وَمِنَ الْمَاءِ الْبَارِدِ .

131

[Transliteration: Allaa-humma innii as-a-luka hubbaka wa-hubba may-yu-hibbuka, wa-hubba 'a-malin yu-qarribu ilaa hubbika. Allaa-humma ij'al hubbaka a-habba ilayya min naf-sii wa-min ah-lii wa-minal maa-il baa-rid.]

O Allah! I beg of Thee Thy love, and the love of him who loveth Thee, and the conduct that will enable me to attain Thy love. O Allah! let Thy love be dearer to me than my self, mine household and water that is cold.

29.

اَللّٰهُمَّ غَشِّنِيْ بِرَحْمَتِكَ وَجَنِّبْنِيْ عَذَابَكَ

[Transliteration: Allaa-humma ghash-shi-nii bi-rah-matika wa-jannib-nii 'a-dhaa-bak.]

O Allah! Cover me with Thy Mercy and save me from Thy punishment.

30.

اَللّٰهُمَّ ثَبِّتْ قَدَمَيَّ يَوْمَ تَزِلُّ فِيْهِ الْاَقْدَامُ

[Transliteration: Allaa-humma thabbit qada-mayya yauma ta-zillu fii-hil aq-daam.]

O Allah! Keep me steadfast when feet begin to waver.

31.

اَللّٰهُمَّ حَاسِبْنِيْ حِسَابًا يَّسِيْرًا

[Transliteration: Allaa-humma haa-sibnii hisaabay yasii-ran.]

O Allah! Judge me leniently (on the Day of Judgement).

132

32.

رَبِّ اغْفِرْ لِيْ خَطِيْئَتِيْ يَوْمَ الدِّيْنِ

[Transliteration: Rabbigh-fir lii khatii-a-tii yaumad diin.]

O Allah! Forgive me my sins on the Day of Requital.

33.

اَللَّهُمَّ قِنِيْ عَذَابَكَ يَوْمَ تَبْعَثُ عِبَادَكَ

[Transliteration: Allaa-humma qinii 'a-dhaa-baka yauma tab'a-thu 'i-baa-dak.]

O Allah! Save me from Thy Chastisement on the day Thou wilt raise up Thy slaves.

34.

اَللَّهُمَّ اِنَّ مَغْفِرَتَكَ اَوْسَعُ مِنْ ذُنُوبِيْ وَرَحْمَتَكَ اَرْجٰى عِنْدِيْ مِنْ عَمَلِيْ

[Transliteration: Allaa-humma inna magh-firataka aw-sa-u min dhu-nuubii wa-rah-mataka arjaa 'indii min 'a-ma-lii.]

O Allah! Verily Thy forgiveness is wider than mine inequities and I have better hope in Thy Mercy than in my conduct.

35.

اَللَّهُمَّ اِنِّيْ اَسْاَلُكَ رِضَاكَ وَالْجَنَّةَ وَاَعُوْذُ بِكَ مِنْ غَضَبِكَ وَالنَّارِ

[Transliteration: Allaa-humma innii as-a-luka ridaaka wal-jannata wa-a-'uudhu bika min gha-dabika wan-naar.]

O Allah! I beg of Thee Thy Good Pleasure and the Garden (i.e., Paradise). I also beg of Thee to spare me out of Thy Mercy Your anger and punishment of the Fire.

133

36.

اَللّٰهُمَّ اِنِّيْ اَعُوْذُ بِرِضَاكَ مِنْ سَخَطِكَ وَبِمُعَافَاتِكَ مِنْ عُقُوْبَتِكَ ،
وَاَعُوْذُ بِكَ مِنْكَ لَا اُحْصِىْ ثَنَاءً عَلَيْكَ اَنْتَ كَمَا اَثْنَيْتَ عَلٰى نَفْسِكَ

[Transliteration: Alla-humma innii a'uu-dhu bi-ridaaka min
sa-kha-tika wa-bi-mu'aa-faatika min 'u-quu-batika, wa-a-'uu-dhu
bika minka laa uh-sii tha-naa-an 'a-layka an-ta kamaa ath-nayta 'a-laa
nafsik.]

O Allah! I seek refuge in Thy good pleasure from Thy displeasure,
and Thy forgiveness from Thy retribution; and I seek refuge in Thee
from Thee. Unable am I to reckon Thy Praise which is Thine. Thou
art, indeed, as Thou hast described Thyself.

37.

اَللّٰهُمَّ اغْفِرْ لِيْ وَارْحَمْنِيْ وَتُبْ عَلَيَّ اِنَّكَ اَنْتَ التَّوَّابُ الرَّحِيْمُ

[Transliteration: Allaa-hummagh-fir lii war-ham-nii wa-tub 'alayya
innaka antat tawwaa-bur rahiim.]

O Allah! Forgive me, be kind to me, have mercy on me. Verily Thou
art Most Kind, Most Merciful.

38.

اَللّٰهُمَّ اَنْتَ رَبِّيْ لَا اِلٰهَ اِلَّا اَنْتَ خَلَقْتَنِيْ وَاَنَا عَبْدُكَ وَاَنَا عَلٰى عَهْدِكَ
وَوَعْدِكَ مَا اسْتَطَعْتُ ، اَعُوْذُ بِكَ مِنْ شَرِّ مَا صَنَعْتُ ، اَبُوْءُ لَكَ
بِنِعْمَتِكَ عَلَيَّ ، وَاَبُوْءُ بِذَنْبِيْ فَاغْفِرْ لِيْ فَاِنَّهُ لَا يَغْفِرُ الذُّنُوْبَ
اِلَّا اَنْتَ .

[Transliteration: Allaa-humma anta rabbii laa ilaaha illaa anta
khalaq-tanii wa-a-na 'abduka wa-a-na 'alaa 'ahdika wa-wa'dika
mas-ta-ta'-tu, a-'oo-dhu bika min sharri maa sa-na'tu, a-buu-u laka

bi-ni'matika 'a-layya, wa-a-buu-u bi-<u>dh</u>am-bii fa<u>gh</u>-fir-lii fa-innahu
laa ya<u>gh</u>-firu<u>dh</u> <u>dh</u>unuu-ba illaa anta.]

O Allah! Thou art my Lord. There is no Allah save Thee. Thou hast
created me and I am Thy slave. And I abide by Thy covenant and
promise as best as I can. I seek refuge in Thee from the mischief of
what I have wrought. I acknowledge unto Thee Thy favour which
Thou hast bestowed upon me and, I confess also my inequity, so,
forgive me for none forgiveth sins save Thee.

39.

اَللّٰهُمَّ اِنِّيْ اَعُوْذُ بِكَ مِنْ شَرِّ سَمْعِيْ وَمِن شَرِّ بَصَرِيْ وَمِنْ شَرِّ لِسَانِيْ
وَمِنْ شَرِّ قَلْبِيْ وَمِنْ شَرِّ مَنِيِّيْ ، وَاَعُوْذُ بِكَ مِنْ عَذَابِ جَهَنَّمَ وَمِنْ
عَذَابِ الْقَبْرِ وَمِنْ فِتْنَةِ الْمَسِيْحِ الدَّجَّالِ ، وَاَعُوْذُ بِكَ مِنْ
فِتْنَةِ الْمَحْيَا وَالْمَمَاتِ .

[Transliteration: Allaa-humma innii a-'oo-<u>dh</u>u bika min <u>sh</u>arri sam'ii
wa-min <u>sh</u>arri ba-<u>s</u>a-rii wa-min <u>sh</u>arri lisaanii wa-min <u>sh</u>arri qalbii
wa-min <u>sh</u>arri ma-niyyatii. Wa-a-'oo-<u>dh</u>u bika min 'a-dhaabi
jahannama wa-min 'a-<u>dh</u>aabil qabri wa-min fitnatil masii-<u>h</u>id
daj-jaali, wa-a-'oo-<u>dh</u>u bika min fitnatil ma<u>h</u>-yaa-ya wal-ma-maat.]

O Allah! I seek refuge in Thee from the mischief of my ears, and from
the mischief of my eyes, and from the mischief of my tongue, and
from the mischief of my heart, and from the mischief of my carnal
desires, and I seek refuge in Thee from the punishment of Hell, and
from the punishment of the grave, and from the calamity of dajjaal
(anti christ), and I seek refuge in Thee from the trials and temptations
of life and death.

40.

اَللّٰهُمَّ اِنِّي اَسْاَلُكَ مِنْ خَيْرِ مَا سَاَلَكَ مِنْهُ نَبِيُّكَ مُحَمَّدُ (صَلَّى اللهُ عَلَيْهِ وَسَلَّمَ) ، وَاَعُوْذُ بِكَ مِنْ شَرِّ مَا اسْتَعَاذَ مِنْهُ نَبِيُّكَ مُحَمَّدُ (صَلَّى اللهُ عَلَيْهِ وَسَلَّمَ) .

[Transliteration: Allaa-humma innii as-a-luka min khayri maa sa-a-laka min-hu nabiy-yuka Muhammadun (Sallallaahu 'Alayhi Wasallam). Wa-a-'uu-dhu bika min sharri mas-ta-'aa-dha-ka minhu nabiy-yuka Muhammadun (Sallallaahu 'Alayhi Wasallam).]

O Allah! I beg of Thee all the good things that Your Prophet Muhammad, [Peace be upon him] had begged of Thee, and I seek Thy refuge from all the evils from which Your Prophet Muhammad, [Peace be upon him] had sought refuge in Thee.

41.

اَللّٰهُمَّ صَلِّ عَلَى مُحَمَّدٍ وَّعَلَى آلِ مُحَمَّدٍ كَمَا صَلَّيْتَ عَلَى اِبْرَاهِيْمَ وَعَلَى آلِ اِبْرَاهِيْمَ اِنَّكَ حَمِيْدٌ مَّجِيْدٌ ، اَللّٰهُمَّ بَارِكْ عَلَى مُحَمَّدٍ وَّعَلَى آلِ مُحَمَّدٍ كَمَا بَارَكْتَ عَلَى اِبْرَاهِيْمَ وَعَلَى آلِ اِبْرَاهِيْمَ اِنَّكَ حَمِيْدٌ مَّجِيْدٌ ، اَللّٰهُمَّ اَنْزِلْهُ الْمَقْعَدَ الْمُقَرَّبَ عِنْدَكَ يَوْمَ الْقِيَامَةِ ، وَاَبْلِغْهُ الْوَسِيْلَةَ وَالدَّرَجَةَ الرَّفِيْعَةَ وَابْعَثْهُ مَقَامًا مَحْمُوْدَانِ الَّذِيْ وَعَدتَّهُ .

[Transliteration: Allaa-humma salli 'a-laa Muhammadiw wa-'a-laa aa-li Muhammadin kamaa sallayta 'a-laa Ibraahiima wa-'a-laa aa-li Ibraahiima innaka hamidum majiid. Allaa-humma baarik 'a-laa Muhammadiw wa-'a-laa aa-li Muhammadin kamaa baarakta 'a-laa Ibraahiima wa-'a-laa aa-li Ibraahiima innka hamidum majiid.

136

Allaa-humma anzilhul maq'a-dal mu-qarraba 'indaka yaumal qiyaamati, wa-abligh-hul wasii-lata wad-daraja-tar rafii-'a-ta wab-'ath-hu maqaamam mah-muda-nil ladhii wa-'ad-tahu.]

O Allah! Magnify Muhammad and his posterity and followers as Thou hast magnified Ibraahiim (Abraham) and his posterity and followers; verily, Thou art the Praiseworthy, the Majestic. O Allah! bless Muhammad and his posterity and followers as Thou hast blest Ibraahiim and his posterity and followers; verily, Thou art the Praiseworthy, the Majestic. O Allah! send him down on the Day of Judgement into the place of special nearness unto Thee, and elevate him to places of honour and intercession, and grant him the place of choicest favour and worthiness Thou hast promised for him.

137

Appendix II

Prayers for particular occasions

MANY PRAYERS FOR SPECIFIC OCCASIONS have, also, been taught to us by the noble Prophet (Peace be upon him). We are reproducing some of them here that are easy to learn and can be made use of by us in our daily life. They should be learnt by heart and recited habitually at moments for which they are indicated.

1. At daybreak:

اَللّٰهُمَّ بِكَ اَصْبَحْنَا وَبِكَ اَمْسَيْنَا وَبِكَ نَحْيٰى وَبِكَ نَمُوْتُ وَاِلَيْكَ الْمَصِيْرُ .

[Transliteration: Allaa-humma bika as-bahnaa wa-bika am-saynaa wa-bika nahyaa wa-bika na-muut wa-ilaykal masiir.]

O Allah! with Thy help do we enter upon the morning, and with Thy help do we enter upon the evening, with Thy help do we live and with Thy help do we die, and unto Thee shall be the resurrection.

2. When evening sets in:

اَللّٰهُمَّ بِكَ اَمْسَيْنَا وَبِكَ اَصْبَحْنَا وَبِكَ نَحْيٰى وَبِكَ نَمُوْتُ وَاِلَيْكَ النُّشُوْرُ .

[Transliteration: Allaa-humma bika am-saynaa wa-bika as-bahnaa wabika nahyaa wa-bika namuut wa-ilaykan nushuur.]

O Allah! with Thy help do we enter upon the evening, and with Thy help do we enter upon the morning, with Thy help do we live and with Thy help do we die, and unto Thee shall be the resurrection.

138

3. On retiring to bed:

اَللّٰهُمَّ بِاسْمِكَ اَمُوْتُ وَاَحْيٰى

[Transliteration: Allaa-humma bi-ismika a-muutu wa-ahyaa.]

O Allah! in Thy name do I live and die.

4. On rising up in the morning:

اَلْحَمْدُ لِلّٰهِ الَّذِيْ اَحْيَانِيْ بَعْدَ مَا اَمَاتَنِيْ وَاِلَيْهِ النُّشُوْرُ

[Transliteration: Alhamdu-lillaahil ladhii ahyaanii ba'da maa a-maa-tanii wa-ilayhin nushuur.]

Praise be to Allah Who restored unto me life, after having caused me to die, and unto Him shall be the resurrection.

5. Before entering the toilet (lavatory):

بِسْمِ اللّٰهِ اَللّٰهُمَّ اِنِّيْ اَعُوْذُ بِكَ مِنَ الْخُبُثِ وَالْخَبَائِثِ

[Transliteration: Bis-mil-laahi allaa-humma innii a-'oo-dhu bika minal khu-bu-thi wal-khabaa-ith.]

In the Name of Allah, O Allah! I seek refuge in Thee from the wicked devils both male and female.

6. On coming out of the toilet (lavatory):

اَلْحَمْدُ لِلّٰهِ الَّذِيْ اَذْهَبَ عَنِّي الْاَذٰى وَعَافَانِيْ

[Transliteration: Alhamdu-lillaa-hil ladhii adh-haba 'an-nil a-dhaa wa-aa-faa-nii.]

Praise be to Allah who relieved me of faeces and gave me health.

139

7. While performing wudu:

اَللَّهُمَّ اغْفِرْ لِيْ ذَنْبِيْ وَوَسِّعْ لِيْ فِيْ دَارِيْ وَبَارِكْ لِيْ فِيْ رِزْقِيْ

[Transliteration: Allaa-hummagh-fir lii dhambii wa-was-si' lii fii daari wa-baarik lii fii rizqii.]

O Allah! forgive me my sins, bless my household and grant auspiciousness and prosperity to my sustenance.

8. After completing wudu:

اَشْهَدُ اَن لَّا اِلَه اِلَّا اللهُ وَحْدَهُ لَا شَرِيْكَ لَهُ وَاَشْهَدُ اَنَّ مُحَمَّدًا عَبْدُهُ وَرَسُوْلُهُ ، اَللَّهُمَّ اجْعَلْنِيْ مِنَ التَّوَّابِيْنَ وَاجْعَلْنِيْ مِنَ الْمُتَطَهِّرِيْنَ .

[Transliteration: Ash-hadu allaa ilaaha illal-laahu wahdahu laa sharika lahu wa-ash-hadu anna Muhammadan 'abduhu wa-rasulu-hu. Allaa-hummaj 'alnii minat taw-waabiina waj'alnii minal muta-tah-hi-riin.]

I bear witness that there is no deity except One Allah. He is alone. He hath no partner. And I bear witness that Muhammad is His slave and His Messenger. O Allah! make me among those that repent and among those that remain clean.

9. Enter the masjid (mosque) with the right foot first and say:

رَبِّ اغْفِرْ لِيْ وَافْتَحْ لِيْ اَبْوَابَ رَحْمَتِكَ

[Transliteration: Rabbigh-fir lii waftah lii abwaa-ba rah-matik.]

O Lord! forgive me my sins and open unto me the gates of Thy Mercy.

10. On coming out of the masjid step out first with the left foot and say:

رَبِّ اغْفِرْ لِيْ وَافْتَحْ لِيْ اَبْوَابَ فَضْلِكَ

[Transliteration: Rabbigh-fir lii waftah lii abwaa-ba fad-lik.]

O Lord! forgive me my sins and open unto me the doors of Thy Bounty.

11. Before commencing to eat:

بِسْمِ اللهِ وَعَلَى بَرَكَةِ اللهِ

[Transliteration: Bismillaahi wa'a-laa ba-ra-katil-laah.]

In the name of Allah and upon the blessings of Allah.

12. At the end of a meal:

اَلْحَمْدُ لِلهِ الَّذِيْ اَطْعَمَنَا وَسَقَانَا وَجَعَلَنَا مِنَ الْمُسْلِمِيْنَ

[Transliteration: Alhamdulillaahil ladhii at-a-manaa wa-saqaa-naa wa-ja-'a-lanaa minal musli-miin.]

Praise be to Allah who fed us and gave us drink and raised us as Muslims.

13. When dining at someone's place:

اَللّٰهُمَّ اَطْعِمْ مَنْ اَطْعَمَنِيْ وَاسْقِ مَنْ سَقَانِيْ

[Transliteration: Alaa-humma at-im man at-a-manii was-qi man saqaa-nii.]

O Allah! feed him who fed me and give him drink who gave me to drink.

14. When riding a beast of burden or a carriage:

اَلْحَمْدُ لِلهِ الَّذِيْ سَخَّرَ لَنَا هٰذَا وَمَا كُنَّا لَهُ مُقْرِنِيْنَ وَاِنَّا اِلٰى رَبِّنَا لَمُنْقَلِبُوْنَ .

[Transliteration: Alhamdu lillaahil ladhii sakh-kha-ra lanaa haa-dhaa wa-maa kunnaa lahu muqri-niina wa-innaa ilaa rabbinaa lamun-qali-buun.

Praise be to Allah! Glory be to Him who hath subjugated it to us though we were unable to subdue it. Behold, we are assuredly to return unto the Lord.

15. When setting forth on a journey:

اَللّٰهُمَّ هَوِّنْ عَلَيْنَا هٰذَا السَّفَرَ وَاطْوِ عَنَّا بُعْدَهُ ، اَللّٰهُمَّ أَنْتَ الصَّاحِبُ فِي السَّفَرِ وَالْخَلِيْفَةُ فِي الْأَهْلِ ، اَللّٰهُمَّ اِنِّي اَعُوْذُ بِكَ مِنْ وَّعْثَاءِ السَّفَرِ وَكَآبَةِ الْمَنْظَرِ وَسُوْءِ الْمُنْقَلَبِ فِي الْمَالِ وَالْأَهْلِ وَالْوَلَدِ .

[Transliteration: Allaa-humma hawwin 'alaynaa haa-dhas safara wat-wi 'annaa bu'dahu. Allaa-humma antas saahibu fis safari wal-khaliifatu fil ahli. Allaa-humma innii a-'oo-dhu bika miw-wa-a'-thaa-is safari wa-ka-aa-batil man-zari wa-suu-il mun-qalabi fil maali wal-ahli wal-walad.]

O Allah! make this journey of ours easy for us and roll up for us the distance thereof. O Allah! Thou art our Companion in the journey and the Caretaker of our household. O Allah! I seek refuge in Thee from the toil of the journey and from beholding a sad sight and a bad reverse in my wealth, household and children.

16. On returning home from a journey:

اٰئِبُوْنَ تَائِبُوْنَ عَابِدُوْنَ لِرَبِّنَا حَامِدُوْنَ

[Transliteration: Aa-i-buun taa-i-buun 'aa-bi-duun li-rabbinaa haami-duun.]

We return unto Allah, penitents, adorers and worshippers of our Lord.

17. When bidding farewell to anyone:

اَسْتَوْدِعُ اللّٰهَ دِيْنَكَ وَاَمَانَتَكَ وَخَوَاتِيْمَ اَعْمَالِكَ

[Transliteration: As-tau-di-'ullaaha dii-naka wa-amaa-nataka wa-kha-waa-tiima 'aa-maalik.]

I place Thee in the hands of Allah, and Thy things that need protection and the end of Thy deeds.

18. On seeing anyone in distress:

اَلْحَمْدُ لِلّٰهِ الَّذِيْ عَافَانِيْ مِمَّا ابْتَلَاكَ بِهِ وَفَضَّلَنِيْ عَلٰى كَثِيْرٍ مِمَّنْ خَلَقَ تَفْضِيْلًا .

[Transliteration: Alhamdu lillaahil ladhii 'aa-faani mim-mab-talaa-ka bihi wa-fad-dalanii 'a-laa ka-thiirim mim-man khalaqa taf-diilan.]

Praise be to Lord who saved me from that which He hath afflicted thee, and made me better than many of His creatures (purely out of His Mercy. I claim no credit for it).

19. On entering a town:

اَللّٰهُمَّ بَارِكْ لَنَا فِيْهَا

[Transliteration: Allaa-humma baarik lanaa fii-haa.]

O Allah! bless this town for us and make it auspicious for us.

20. When rising from company:

سُبْحَانَكَ اللّٰهُمَّ وَبِحَمْدِكَ لَا اِلٰهَ اِلَّا اَنْتَ ، اَسْتَغْفِرُكَ وَاَتُوبُ اِلَيْكَ

[Transliteration: Subhaa-nakal laahumma wa-bihamdika laa ilaaha illaa an-ta, as-tagh-firuka wa-a-tuubu i-layk.]

143

O Allah! Glory be to Thee, I celebrate Thy praises; There is no Lord save Thee, I beg Thy forgiveness and I repent unto Thee.

وما توفيقي إلا بالله عليه توكلت وإليه انيب

وصلى الله على سيدنا محمد النبي الامي وعلى آله وأصحابه أجمعين ، والحمد لله رب العالمين

Glossary

Abu Daawuud (Musnad), Book on ahaadii<u>th</u> (traditions).

a<u>h</u>aadi<u>th</u>, traditions: Sayings of the Prophet (Peace be upon him) sing. hadii<u>th</u>.

Allah, Name of the Supreme Being Who has no partner and Who is the only One worthy of worship.

Allahu Akbar, Allah is Great.

'Ar<u>sh</u>, The Throne of Allah.

barza<u>kh</u>, Interval period between death and the Day of Judgement.

Bayhaqii, Book on ahaadii<u>th</u> (traditions).

Daarimii, Book on ahaadii<u>th</u> (traditions).

Dajjaal, An imposter, defrauder and liar, who will show great miracles, make dead people alive, etc. He will be killed by 'Eesa (Jesus) (Peace be upon him). The Anti-Christ.

<u>dh</u>ikr, Remembrance of Allah.

dirham, Monetary coinage in the early period of Islaam.

du'aa, Supplication to Allah.

durood, Invoking blessings of Allah on the Prophet (Peace be upon him).

far<u>d</u>, An obligatory act.

Fir'aun, Pharoah. Title of the kings of Egypt.

Haa-maan, Name of a minister of Pharoah.

<u>h</u>adii<u>th</u>, tradition: Saying of the Prophet (Peace be upon him). pl. ahaadi<u>th</u>

<u>h</u>ajj, Pilgrimage to Makkah in Saudi Arabia.

<u>h</u>ouris, Celestial brides of Heaven.

Ibn Maajah, Book on ahaadii<u>th</u> (traditions).

In-<u>Sh</u>a-Allah, If Allah Willing.

isti<u>gh</u>faar, Repentance: seeking forgiveness from Allah.

jihaad, The striving in the Path of Allah, also an Islaamic war.

jihaad akbar, The great striving in the Path of Allah.

Ka'bah, Lit. The symbolic House of Allah in Makkah, Saudi Arabia.

kalimah, The utterance and confession of the creed, i.e. Oneness of Allah.

masjid, Mosque: Muslim place of congregational prayer.

masaajid, Plural of mosque.

Muslim, Believer in the Islaamic faith; also a Book on ahaadii<u>th</u> (traditions.)

145

Musnad Ahmad, Book on ahaadiith (traditions).

Nasa-ee, Book on ahaadiith (traditions).

pilo, Roots and branches of a tree used for cleansing teeth.

Qaa-ruun, Korah, minister of Pharoah.

qudsii (hadiith), Tradition that gives the spoken Words of Allah.

raa-ee, (Sinapis Remosa), kind of mustard seed.

rak'ah, Portion of salaah (prayer).

Ramadaan, Month of fasting. The 9th month of the Islaamic calendar.

ruku', Bowing before Allah during salaah (prayers).

sajdah, Prostrating before Allah during salaah (prayers).

salaah, Islaamic manner of prayers.

saum, Fasting

Sayyid, Title of honour or a member of the family of the Prophet.

Sayyidina, Title of honour of the Prophet and his companions.

Sayyiditina, Title of honour for female companions of the Prophet.

Sayyidul Istighfaar, Chief of the utterings of repentance.

Sharhus Sunnah, A book on ahaadiith (traditions)

sharii'ah, Islaamic law.

Shaykh, Title for a learned person; elderly person; clan.

shirk, Ascribing a partner unto Allah.

surah, Chapter of the Qur-aan.

Taa-if, City near Makkah in Saudi Arabia.

tabliigh, Propagation of Islaam.

tahajjud, Late night voluntary prayers.

taubah, Repentance.

Tirmidhii, A book on ahaadiith (traditions)

Ubai bin Khalaf, Name of arch enemy of the Prophet (Peace be upon him).

Uhud, Mountain north of the city of Madiinah, Saudi Arabia.

ummah, Followers of the Prophet (Peace be upon him).

wudu, Ritual ablution before salaah (prayer) and other devotions.

zakaah, Alms, two and half percent given annually to stipulated persons.

zaqqum, Tree in Hell, fruit of which will be eaten by inmates of Hell.

Index

aright:
    all my states 128
    my faith 129
    my hereafter 129
    my world 129
auspiciousness 10, 13, 31, 40, 103, 122, 140

B

backbiting 29, 53
barzakh 84, 87, 94
beast 28, 141
bedrock 7
benediction 31
benevolence 13, 24, 30, 90, 106, 108, 118
beseech 19, 105, 109
biological 27
blessed 5, 14, 18, 24, 30, 32, 36, 59, 60, 77, 82, 120   blest 18, 137
bondsman/men 24, 27, 67, 68, 95, 97, 120
boons 19, 34
bribery 37, 39
Bukhaa-rii:
    departments of faith 2,
    remove all impurities and sins 10,
    reward of salaah in congregation 11
    the fire of hell forbidden ... 5,

C

character 54
charitable/charity 22, 24-26, 40, 50, 51, 61
chastisement 9, 23, 28, 60, 66, 85, 92, 93, 97, 114, 133
companion 3, 10, 25, 33, 34, 35, 39, 45, 46, 49-51, 53, 54, 58, 67, 68, 71, 75,
        77, 87, 88, 90, 111, 142
compassion 19, 42, 45, 59, 60
conduct 2, 5, 8, 10, 24, 36, 44, 48, 49, 55, 63, 70, 75, 87, 95, 115, 129, 132, 133
congregation 10, 11

148

E

elevated 16
elixir 20, 122
embezzlement 37
embrace 7
encroach 53
essence 3, 17, 95, 105
eternal bliss 85
excellent 2, 10, 70, 95, 99
exclusively 5, 27
extraordinary 24

F

Faith:
    constancy 75, 77
faithful/ly 2, 4, 9, 31, 38, 44, 47, 68, 76, 92, 111, 117, 121
fard 106
fast, see saum
favour 24, 33, 82, 92, 107, 119, 127, 135, 137
felicity 8, 91, 96
Fir'aun 8
Fire 5, 23, 28, 33, 39, 41, 46, 60, 65, 67, 91-93, 123, 124, 133
forgive 19, 59, 76, 79, 110, 115, 116, 118, 119, 124, 125, 128, 133-135, 140, 141
forgiveness 19, 21, 53, 59, 114-119, 121, 126-129, 133, 134, 144
forgiveth 119, 135
fortunate 9, 35, 51
fraud 37-39
Friends of Allah 34
fundamental 22, 30, 32, 37, 66
futile 97, 102, 103, 107

G

gracious 61, 106, 110, 127
gratitude 19, 109
guidance 4, 5, 44, 47, 49, 68, 69, 71-73, 76, 78, 103, 109, 113, 122, 129

guide 51, 52, 68, 101, 104, 131

H

Haa-maan 8

hadiith:

    constancy in devotion 75

    du'aa (supplication) 105, 106

    durood 110

    falsehood/lie 29, 38, 46, 56, 88

    good manners 48, 54, 55

    hajj (pilgrimage) 30, 31, 32, 45

    heaven/paradise 31, 45-48, 51, 54, 56, 61, 82, 92, 98, 119

    hell/fire 5, 23, 28, 36, 38, 39, 40, 45, 53, 61, 65, 67, 79, 87, 93

    honesty/trustworthy 42

    jihaad 65, 79, 118

    kalimah 5, 98, 99, 118

    kindness 59

    martyrdom 43, 81, 82

    monetary dealings 38, 42

    neighbours 50, 51

    piety 61

    prayer-formulas 2

    salaah (prayers) 11, 12, 32, 41, 50, 51, 53, 57, 74, 101

    saum (fasting) 27, 28, 29, 32

    spending in the path of Allah 26

    taubah (repentance) 115, 118, 119, 120

    usury 39

    zakaah 23, 26, 32

hajj 30-32, 45, 66, 74, 79, 86, 91

Heaven 4, 45, 46, 48, 50, 51, 81, 87, 90-94, 98, 119

Hell 4, 5, 9, 23, 36, 38-40, 45, 46, 50, 53, 60, 61, 79, 85, 87, 90-94, 109, 117, 135

hereafter 5, 11, 23, 25, 26, 28, 30, 34-36, 40, 42, 61, 72, 75, 81, 82, 85, 94, 101,
    107, 108, 113, 117, 123, 126, 129, 130

houris 92

humble/ness 12, 20, 62, 99

hypocrite 38, 56, 57, 61

litigation 37, 39, 40
logical 4
Lord 1, 2, 5, 9, 13-19, 21, 24, 25, 28, 31, 33, 34, 36, 37, 40, 41, 43-45, 48, 52,
    64, 67, 75, 76, 81-83, 85, 86, 87, 90-93, 97-100, 105, 110, 114-116, 118,
    119, 123, 124-128, 135, 140-144

M

Madiinah 31, 32, 38
magnificence 12, 16, 17, 104, 108
magnify/ied 19, 109, 111, 112, 137
Majestic 18, 19, 111, 137
Makkah 8, 31, 32, 71, 77
martyrs 42, 81
masjid 10, 11, 31, 140
master 5, 13, 44, 45, 52, 53, 64, 88, 116
memorise 102
mercy 18, 19, 25, 46, 52, 58, 59, 77, 106, 114-117, 125-128, 130, 132-134, 140, 143
misdeeds 19, 94, 107
monetary 37, 42, 43, 59, 122
moral 29, 46, 54, 55, 60, 61, 63, 66, 68-71, 73, 102, 121
mosque, see masjid
Muhammad (Peace be upon him)1, 4, 5, 7, 18, 19, 43, 48, 52, 68,
    84, 85, 91, 109, 111-113, 136, 137, 140
Musaa (Moses) (Peace be upon him) 2, 3, 76, 97-99
Muslim 1, 2, 4, 5, 7-11, 22, 26, 27, 32, 37, 39, 44, 47, 50, 52, 53-55, 61-63, 67
    69-71, 78, 79, 84, 96, 110, 116, 117, 121, 126, 131
Musnad Ahmad:
    five daily prayers obligatory 13
    keep on refreshing your faith 8,
    whoever will offer salaah properly 8

N

Nasa-ee:
    most excellent prayer-formula 2
Nourisher 1

154

nutshell 2, 47

O

obedience 1, 2, 45
obligation 7, 30, 35, 50, 109
obligatory 5, 12, 27, 30, 68, 79, 96, 106, 122
omnipotence 106, 108
Oneness 1, 7
orphan 51

P

Pharaoh, see Fir'aun
pauper 53
piety 7, 28, 29, 33-36, 58, 61, 66, 93, 117, 131
pilgrimage 30-32
pilgrimage, see hajj
pillars of Islaam, see: kalimah; salaah; saum; zakaah; hajj
pilo 40
pious 18, 34, 68, 72, 73, 117, 122
Place of Reckoning 53
pledge 3, 5
posterity 18, 19, 111, 137
praiseworthy 18, 19, 111, 137
prayer 2, 10-13, 18, 19, 21-23, 40, 41, 50, 51, 53, 54, 55, 57, 63, 72, 74, 96,
        105-109, 114, 118, 119, 122, 123, 126, 138
promotes 7, 28, 98
prophet/s 1-5, 7, 8, 10, 12, 18-20, 22, 23, 25-27, 29-32, 34, 35, 36-43, 45-56,
        58-61, 63, 64, 66-68, 70-73, 75, 76, 77-79, 81, 82, 84, 85, 87-89, 92-95,
        97-101, 103, 105-107, 109-113, 118, 119, 121, 122, 136, 138
Prophet Daawuud (David) 42
Prophet Muhammad 1, 4, 5, 7, 52, 68, 84, 85, 109, 111, 113, 136
Prophet Musaa (Moses) 2, 76
propitiating 27
prosperity 24, 26, 40, 140
prostration, see sajdah

155

provocation 60

punishment 9, 23, 24, 33, 35, 36, 60, 67, 72, 73, 74, 76, 82, 85, 88-90, 93, 94, 117, 132, 133, 135

Q

Qaa-ruun 8

qudsii (hadii_th) 98

Qur-aan:

    constancy 75

    courage 76

    Day of Recompence 86

    death 85

    _dhikr (remembrance) 95, 96, 97

    du'aa 105

    durood 109

    fulfilling promises 56

    gentleness of speech 61

    _hajj (pilgrimage) 30

    heaven/paradise 90, 91

    hell/fire 91, 92

    honesty/trustworthy in monetary dealings 37, 38

    humility 61

    jihaad 79

    justice 87, 58, 89

    Last Day 86

    Love of Allah 66

    martyrdom 81

    patience 62, 63

    perseverance 77

    piety and righteousness 33, 34

    preaching and propagation 69

    reward for zakaah 25

    rights of children 46

    rights of husband and wife 47

    rights of neighbours 49

    _salaah (prayers) 12

    _saum (fasting) 27

S

sacred 7, 8, 38, 40, 53, 54, 61, 68, 81, 93, 94, 109, 119
sacrifice/s 27, 67, 72, 77
safeguard 129
Sahiih Muslim:
    Allah removes all impurities 10
    forbidden the fire of Hell 5
    offer prayers in congregation 11
    separates a believer from infidelity 8
    seventy departments of faith 2
sajdah 9, 12, 17
salaah 7-13, 16-20, 22, 27, 31, 32, 36, 41, 66, 72, 96, 101, 103, 106, 111, 122
salutation 31, 90, 111
salvation 1, 5, 6, 8, 41, 45, 56, 59, 113, 116
saum 27, 28, 32, 66
Sayyidina 'Abdullah bin 'Umar 97
Sayyidina 'Abdullah bin Busr 98
Sayyidina 'Abdullah bin Mas'ood 103
Sayyidina 'Alii 100
Sayyidina Abu Hurairah 64, 98, 101
Sayyidina Abu Umaamah 103
Sayyidina Anas 5
Sayyidina Jaabir 98
Sayyidina Mu'aadh 5
Sayyidina Samurah bin Jundub 99
Sayyiditina Faatimah 100
Sayyidul Istighfaar 119
Sharhus Sunnah:
    Laa ilaaha illallaah placed on the balance (scale) 3
sharii'ah 4, 5, 71
shield 28
shirk (making a partner unto Allah) 24
sick 51, 106
sickness 1
sin/s 7, 10, 13, 19, 27, 29, 31, 36, 43, 45, 46, 52, 53, 55, 59, 61, 62, 73, 76,
    79,98,101, 106, 107, 110, 113-119, 122, 124, 125, 133, 135, 140, 141
slander 29, 53, 55

U

Ubai bin Khalaf 8
ummah 70, 77
'umrah 31
unity 1, 3, 5, 63
usurpation 39
usury 37, 39

V

virtue 3, 8, 32, 35, 42, 43, 47, 61, 72, 100, 101, 103, 110, 113, 121

W

weighing 37
Will of Allah 4, 28, 62, 63, 105
worship 1-3, 5, 7, 14, 17, 19, 20, 25, 27, 44, 45, 80, 99, 100, 101, 103, 105-107,
    118, 122, 123, 131
wudu 12, 13, 104, 140

Z

zakaah:
    evasion of zakaah 23, 24
    on one-fortieth of wealth 24
    reward on zakaah 24
    those who do not pay zakaah 23
zaqqum 91, 94

Arabic font: Lamees G̲haamiq (Bold) 14/22

English fonts: Palatino Roman 10/13
                Palatino Italic 10/13
                Palatino Bold
                Helevetica Narrow
                Helevetica Black Normal

Setting on: 'Al-Arabi Linnas̲hr'